DATE DUE

JUN 1 '77			
MAY 2 9 '79			
DEC 3 1985			
JAN 2 3 1986			
MAR 9 1987			
MAR 2 1 1988			
FEB 1 6 1990			

DEMCO 38-297

THE VERSAILLES TREATY

At eleven o'clock on the morning of November 11, 1918, fighting ceased on the western front in France and Belgium. For almost four years the world had watched the bloodiest and most expensive war in history. Now, at last, the return of a peace so desperately desired became a reality.

Two months later the representatives of the victorious powers gathered in Paris to write the treaties of peace. The most important of these agreements was the first to be completed. In less than four months the representatives of the German government were summoned to a suburb of Paris. There, in the Hall of Mirrors in the great palace of the French kings, they signed the documents that formally brought World War I to an end. The Versailles Palace thus gave its name to one of the most famous treaties in history.

This book attempts briefly to tell the story of that treaty. It examines some of the relationships established between leaders such as Woodrow Wilson, David Lloyd George, and Georges Clemenceau, which were not only fascinating in themselves, but tell us much about the spirit of the times. The treaty provisions clearly show the bitter struggle between idealists seeking a just and lasting peace and those more concerned with vengeance and assurances of national security.

Out of the Versailles Treaty came the League of Nations, one of mankind's attempts to find a means of abolishing war. However, the treaty also brought about conditions that helped Adolf Hitler rise to power in Germany, and played a significant role in causing World War II only twenty years later. It would be impossible to choose a single official document that has had more influence on the shaping of events in the years between the two world wars than did the Versailles Treaty.

PRINCIPALS

WOODROW WILSON (1856–1924), president of the United States
DAVID LLOYD GEORGE (1863–1945), prime minister of Great Britain
GEORGES CLEMENCEAU [*klem*-on-so] (1841–1929), premier of France
VITTORIO EMANUELE ORLANDO (1860–1952), premier of Italy
ULRICH VON BROCKDORFF-RANTZAU (1869–1928), German foreign minister and leader of Germany's delegation to Versailles

ALL MERCHANDISE ADVERTISED IN THE TRIBUNE IS GUARANTEED

New York Tribune

First to Last—the Truth: News - Editorials - Advertisements

WEATHER
Fair to-day; to-morrow snow, diminishing northwest to north winds.
Full Report on Page 6

Vol. LXXVII No. 25,987 [Copyright 1918—The Tribune Ass'n] WEDNESDAY, JANUARY 9, 1918 ONE CENT In Greater New York | TWO CENTS Within Commuting Distance | THREE CENTS Elsewhere

Wilson Proclaims America's Peace Plan To Make All the World Free and Safe

President Champions The Russian Cause

Wilson's Terms Guarantee Future, Separate Peace or No

Attitude Different From Lloyd George's

Speech May Be Designed to Correct British Diplomatic Blunder

By C. W. Gilbert

WASHINGTON, Jan. 8.—President Wilson went unexpectedly up to the Capitol to-day and addressed Congress upon the aims of this country in the war. His purpose to speak became known only an hour or two before.

For the first time this country committed itself in favor of the restoration of Alsace-Lorraine to France, the return of Italian provinces of Austria to Italy, an independent Poland and a fairly detailed settlement of the Balkan and Turkish questions. In addition, Mr. Wilson declared for the evacuation of Russian territory, apparently no matter what concessions Germany extorts from Russia, and adopted as the first condition of peace the immensely radical proposal of publicity in all diplomatic arrangements.

In the opinion of Washington, Mr. Wilson's speech is the final and definite statement of the purposes of the nations which are fighting Germany, to which they will hold to the end unless they grow weary of waiting while American preparations become slowly effective.

Principle Admits Of No Compromise

There is room left by the President for trading with Germany on details, for no language could be so explicit as to exclude all bargaining, but a principle which admits of no compromise underlies every one of the terms the President lays down. The President defines that principle thus: "Justice to all peoples and nationalities and their right to live on equal terms of liberty and safety with one another, whether they be strong or weak."

Applying that principle, the President outlines more definite conditions of peace than did Lloyd George in his last speech, laying emphasis, as he always does, upon the international and idealistic elements in the problem more strongly than did the British Premier.

It is thought that the President's address will be less agreeable to Germany than Lloyd George's. An example of the difference in sharpness with which the Allied terms were stated by the spokesman of the two nations and the smaller room that is left for bargaining by the American President is furnished by the treatment of Alsace-Lorraine.

Definite Demand for Restoration of Alsace

Lloyd George had said that there must be a "reconsideration of the great wrong of 1871." Mr. Wilson says "the wrong done to France by Prussia in 1871, in the matter of Alsace-Lorrane, should be righted." The difference in explicitness that lies in those two expressions run all through the two speeches. No uterance of the President's evoked a response equal to that which followed his declartion regarding Alsace-Lorraine. The combined houses of Congress rose to their feet and cheered. Even over Belgium less feeling was shown than over France. It was one of the striking incidents of the day.

Coming as it does right after the British definition of terms the President's address has contributed to the talk of peace that has been heard recently in Washington. Men say that the action of the Allies in stating at last their aims in detail indicates a belief among the governments that Germany is about ready to make a serious move for peace.

Mr. Wilson's utterance, following Lloyd George's so closely as it does, looks like concerted action among the opponents of the Central Powers to lay all their cards on the table.

Though this view was expressed today no one was to be found who could see the hope of early peace in the conditions the President laid down. Granted a free hand in Russia Germany might agree to the reparation and restoration in the West and to concessions to Italy, but the President's speech closes the door to Germany in Russia just as effectively as in the West.

Differs With Lloyd George On Russian Question

It is precisely here that Mr. Wilson differs most strikingly from Lloyd George. The British Premier slurred over the Russian situation. He held out no hope to those in Russia who are

Continued on Third Page

Trotzky Arrives At Brest-Litovsk To Renew Parley

LONDON, Jan. 8.—The Russian peace delegation, including Foreign Minister Trotzky, reached Brest-Litovsk on Monday for the reopening of negotiations that afternoon, according to a Berlin dispatch received in Copenhagen and forwarded by the Exchange Telegraph Company.

Count Adam Tarnowski von Tarnow, according to a dispatch to the Berlin "Tageblatt" received in Amsterdam, has been appointed an Austrian delegate to the peace conference at Brest-Litovsk. The count was named ambassador to the United States last spring, but was never officially received by the American government.

Three members of the Persian parliament accompanied Talat Bey, the Turkish Grand Vizier, when he arrived in Berlin for conferences on the war situation.

British Terms Denounced by Enemy Press

Premier's Speech Generally Ridiculed; "Vorwaerts" Not Heard From

LONDON, Jan. 8.—Although no statement by the leading German Socialist daily "Vorwaerts," has been received, all the other comment of enemy countries on Lloyd George's speech of Friday, outlining Great Britain's war aims condemns the Premier's stand.

It is declared by the German and Austrian press that the position of the Prime Minister has moderated, but the change is said to be not great enough to furnish a ground for a settlement.

The "Norddeutsche Allgemeine Zeitung," the semi-official German organ, accordings to an Amsterdam dispatch, says:

"Even if David Lloyd George now, for obvious reasons, renounces the talk about all kinds of crushing aims with which he formerly was wont to make an impression on the masses of his own people and the Allies, and if those points in which Russia had the greatest interest were erased from the general programme of the Entente, there nevertheless has been virtually no change in England's own war aims. They are, as before, the result of the will for unrestricted world power.

"Mr. Lloyd George knows to-day, as when he m. ʃ. his first war speech, that the territorial integrity of the Austro-Hungarian monarchy, as wel as that of the other allies of Germany, must form the cornerstone in the building of a new peace. Nevertheless, he adheres to his imperialistic war aims with their unmeasured demands, and only by a change in tone tries to give the impression that he takes into account the alteration of the military and political situation. It is characteristic of him and his allies."

Maximilian Harden, in "Die Zukunft," according to an Amsterdam dispatch, scathingly condemns Austro-German plans for annexations in the East.

He declares that a broad chasm still yawns between the two parties at Brest-Litovsk, and that if the demands of the Central Powers to annex or join the territories in question to the two empires in Europe are realized, then there will again be only an armistice and there will be no lasting and honorable peace with Russia, which country will not eternally wear Lenine's red livery, or be satisfied with the disintegration and communistic dwarfing of communities.

"Washington Holds Key"

Herr Harden says that even were the Letts, Lithuanians, Livonians and Esthonians, who for five centuries have been opposed to all Germanism, to vote contrary to all expectations, for union with the German Empire, Germany would be obliged to refuse that union, for its body cannot bear fresh foreign elements, and it does not desire, by provoking the deep hostility of the Russian people, which before 1950 will compromise 200,000,000 souls, to brew a consoling draft for its Western enemies.

The key to the Temple of Peace, Herr Harden declares, lies in the Capitol at Washington.

The "Koelnische Zeitung" says:

"If Lloyd George's war aims should be fulfilled Germany would be driven back into her position in 1914 but without Alsace-Lorraine and the German colonies and loaded with an immense war indemnity, faced with a dangerous Polish state on her frontier, and, moreover, delivered to the discretion of the Entente Allies for receiving goods. The peace offer of Premier Lloyd George cannot be accepted."

The Fourteen Conditions

1—Open covenants of peace, openly arrived at, after which there shall be no private international understandings.

2—Absolute freedom of the seas, alike in peace and in war, except as they may be closed by international action.

3—The removal of all economic barriers and the establishment of an equality of trade conditions among all the nations consenting to the peace.

4—Adequate guarantees that national armaments will be reduced to the lowest point consistent with domestic safety.

5—A free, open-minded and absolutely impartial adjustment of all colonial claims, based upon the principle that the interests of the populations must have equal weight with the equal claims of the government concerned.

6—The evacuation of all Russian territory and such a settlement of all Russian questions as will secure for her unhampered opportunity for independent political development and national policy.

7—The evacuation and restoration of Belgium, without any attempt to limit her sovereignty.

8—The liberation of all French territory and the restoration of the invaded portions, and the righting of the wrong done to France by Prussia in 1871 in the matter of Alsace-Lorraine.

9—The readjustment of the frontiers of Italy along clearly recognizable lines of nationality.

10—The freest opportunity of the peoples of Austria-Hungary for autonomous development.

11—The evacuation of Rumania, Serbia and Montenegro, with free access to the sea for Serbia; the restoration of occupied territories; the fixing of the relations of the several Balkan states along historically established lines of allegiance and nationality, and international guarantees of their political and economic independence and territorial integrity.

12—Secure sovereignty for the Turkish portions of the present Ottoman Empire, but with assurance that the other nationalities now under Turkish rule shall have unmolested opportunity of autonomous development; the Dardanelles to be permanently opened to all nations under international guarantees.

13—Erection of an independent Polish state, including the territories inhabited by indisputably Polish populations, with free access to the sea and with political and economic independence and territorial integrity internationally guaranteed.

14—The formation of a general association of nations under specific covenants for the purpose of affording mutual guarantees of political independence and territorial integrity to great and small states alike.

WILSON'S HANDWRITING ON MITTELEUROPA

By Frank H. Simonds

THE President's peace terms require three stupendous concessions on the part of Germany. They demand that she shall consent to the destruction of her great scheme of Mitteleuropa; that she and her allies shall surrender 210,000 square miles of conquered territory, inhabited by 40,000,000, an area greater than that of Germany before the war and a population in excess of that of France in 1911, and, finally, that Germany, Austria and Turkey shall cede territory in their possession when the war broke out. Actually the President asks greater sacrifices of Germany than victorious Europe asked and France had to make after Waterloo and at the Congress of Vienna.

Looked at from the point of view of the Mitteleuropa scheme, the President's terms cuts this grandiose creation by restoring uRmania and Serbia and bestowing upon the latter a seacoast, obviously in Albania. It was to break down such a barrier that Austria, at Germany's direction, assailed Serbia in July, 1914, and produced the World War. When Serbia and Rumania have been restored Bulgaria and Turkey will be cut off from Austria and Germany.

But the amputation at the waist, if one may use this figure, is accompanied by similar operations on all four limbs. Of the two arms of Mitteleuropa, that extending westward through Belgium to the coast is eliminated by the restoration of Belgium, that which extends eastward to Riga is cut off by the creation of a free Poland, having Danzig as a seaport, and by the restoration to Russia of the remainder of Russian lands conquered by the Germans and the Austrians. In the same way, by depriving the Turk of his Mesopotamian and Syrian lands, as well as his Armenian provinces, President Wilson takes off both legs.

But the President does not stop there. He not only insists upon the restitution by Germany and Austria of all the lands taken in the present war; he demands that Germany shall cede Alsace-Lorraine to France and the Polish districts of Prussia to the new Poland. By these two cessions Germany would lose more than 12,800 square miles and between 5,000,000 and 6,000,000 of people which were hers before the present war. Austria would, in the same fashion, have to give up Trieste and the Trentino, with nearly a million people and four or five thousand square miles, as well as the Polish half of Silesia, containing 6,000,000 people.

Finally, Turkey under the President's proposal would lose Arabia, Armenia, Syria, Palestine and Mesopotamia. That is about one-half of the Turkish Empire and no less than 7,000,000 people—a full third of the population of the empire. Turkey would be restricted to the Anatolian district, in which the Osmanli element predominates, and he would lose his hold upon the holy cities of Mecca, Medina and Jerusalem.

President Wilson has gone far beyond Lloyd George in the matter of Poland, Russia and Austria-Hungary. He has reëchoed the British Prime Minister's terms in the Balkans, in Asiatic Turkey, in Belgium and in the matter of Alsace-Lorraine and the Italian Irredenta.

In sum, in the present war Germany and her allies have conquered 120,000 square miles of Russian territory, 7,000 square miles of French territory, 12,000 square miles of Belgian territory (with Luxemburg included), 40,000 square miles of Serbian and Montenegrin territory, 35,000 square miles of Rumanian territory and 6,000 square miles of Greek and Albanian soil. A total area of 210,000 square miles, about equal to that of Germany, has been taken by the Kaiser and his allies, together with a population of 40,000,000.

Fourteen Definite Aims Laid Down

Germany Must Restore Belgium, Right the Wrong Done to France in '71 and Evacuate All Occupied Territory Taken From Russia

Diplomacy Shall Be Open; No Trade Boycott After War

Freedom of Seas, Reduction of Armaments, Liberation of Poland and of Nations Under Turks Required—League of Nations to Enforce Treaty

WASHINGTON, Jan. 8.—With only an hour's notice, President Wilson appeared before Congress to-day to restate the war aims of the United States and to lay down fourteen conditions which he considers essential for a lasting peace. He said:

"Gentlemen of the Congress:

"Once more, as repeatedly before, the spokesmen of the Central Empires have indicated their desire to discuss the objects of the war and the possible basis of a general peace. Parleys have been in progress at Brest-Litovsk between Russian representatives and representatives of the Central Powers, to which the attention of all the belligerents has been invited, for the purpose of ascertaining whether it may be possible to extend these parleys into a general conference with regard to terms of peace and settlement.

"The Russian representatives presented not only a perfectly definite statement of the principles upon which they would be willing to conclude peace, but also an equally definite programme of the concrete application of those principles. The representatives of the Central Powers, on their part, presented an outline of settlement which, if much less definite, seemed susceptible of liberal interpretation until their specific programme of practical terms was added. That programme proposed no concessions at all, either to the sovereignty of Russia or to the preferences of the populations with whose fortunes it dealt, but meant, in a word, that the Central Empires were to keep every foot of territory their armed forces had occupied—every province, every city, every point of vantage—as a permanent addition to their territories and their power.

Russia Cannot Entertain Such Proposals of Conquest

"It is a reasonable conjecture that the general principles of settlement which they at first suggested originated with the more liberal statesmen of Germany and Austria, the men who have begun to feel the force of their own people's thought and purpose, while the concrete terms of actual settlement came from the military leaders, who have no thought but to keep what they have got. The negotiations have been broken off. The Russian representatives were sincere and in earnest. They cannot entertain such proposals of conquest and domination.

"The whole incident is full of significance. It is also full of perplexity. With whom are the Russian representatives dealing? For whom are the representatives of the Central Empires speaking? Are they speaking for the majorities of their respective Parliaments or for the minority parties, that military and imperialistic minority which has so far dominated their whole policy and controlled the affairs of Turkey and the Balkan States, which have felt obliged to become their associates in this war?

"The Russian representatives have insisted, very justly, very wisely, and in the true spirit of modern democracy, that the conferences they have been holding with the Teutonic and Turkish statesmen should be held within open, not closed, doors, and all the world has been audience, as was desired. To whom have we been listening, then? To those who speak the spirit and intention of the resolutions of the German Reichstag of the 9th of July last, the spirit and intention of the Liberal leaders and parties of Germany, or to those who resist and defy that spirit and intention and insist upon conquest and subjugation? Or are we listening, in fact, to both, unreconciled and in open and hopeless contradiction? These are very serious and pregnant questions. Upon the answer to them depends the peace of the world.

No Confusion of Counsel Among Adversaries of Germany

"But, whatever the results of the parleys at Brest-Litovsk, whatever the confusions of counsel and of purpose in the utterances of the spokesmen of the Central Empires, they have again attempted to acquaint the world with their objects in the war and have again challenged their adversaries to say what their objects are and what sort of settlement they would deem just and satisfactory. There is no

THE VERSAILLES TREATY

1919
Germany's Formal Surrender at the End of the Great War

By Harold Cecil Vaughan

A World Focus Book

FRANKLIN WATTS, INC.
NEW YORK | 1975

Dedicated to my niece
Diane Vaughan Brophy

Photograph on title page (courtesy *New York Public Library Picture Collection*) shows the front page of the *New York Tribune* on January 9, 1918, the day after President Woodrow Wilson delivered his famous speech to Congress outlining Fourteen Points to bring peace to the world after World War I. Point 14 called for the formation of a League of Nations, Wilson's cherished dream.

Photographs courtesy of: European Picture Service: pp. vi, 40 top, 61 top; German Information Center: pp. 7 bottom, 31; Library of Congress: pp. 34 top, 40 bottom, 45, 52 bottom; New York Public Library Picture Collection: title; United Nations: p. 34 bottom; U.S. Signal Corps: pp. 7 top, 14, 19, 22, 52 top, 61 bottom.

Cover design by Nick Krenitsky
Map by George Buctel

Library of Congress Cataloging in Publication Data

Vaughan, Harold Cecil.
   The Versailles treaty, 1919.

   (A World focus book)
   SUMMARY: Discusses the drafting, approval, signing, and deeply felt effects of the Treaty of Versailles, one of the most famous treaties in history.
   Bibliography: p.
   1. Versailles, Treaty of, June 28, 1919. (Germany)—Juvenile literature. 2. Paris. Peace Conference, 1919—Juvenile literature. [1. Versailles, Treaty of, June 28, 1919 (Germany) 2. Paris. Peace Conference, 1919] I. Title.
D643.A7V36   940.3′144   74–8865
ISBN 0–531–02783–X

Contents

Prologue 1

The Organization of
the Paris Conference 9

The Big Four 16

The Territorial Provisions
of the Treaty 25

Military Restrictions,
Economic Provisions,
and Reparations 36

The League of Nations 41

The German Response 46

Conclusion 57

Bibliography 64

Index 65

Soldiers on the front line hear
the news that World War I is over.

Prologue

A world tired of suffering and death greeted the end of the Great War, as World War I was then called, with hysterical laughter and tears. Its exact cost in lives and money would never be known, but it was already clear that in the course of its 1,565 days (1914–18) this was the bloodiest and most expensive war in history. Directly or indirectly every corner of the globe had been affected. Of the more than 65 million men mobilized, 13 million died in action or later of wounds. Some 22 million others were wounded, just under a third of those being permanently disabled. It was estimated that more than double the number of men died in World War I than in all of the major wars since the start of the Napoleonic conquests in 1790, including the devastating American Civil War!

The total net direct cost of conducting the war was later placed at $186 billion (which would be approximately five times as much, or $930 billion, at today's dollar value) to which must be added property damage of $37 billion and production losses of $45 billion. War relief and losses suffered by neutrals added $2 billion more, bringing the total real economic cost to $270 billion. Even that amount ignored the $67 billion that was the coldly calculated, capitalized value of all human lives lost as a direct result of the war. That would bring the grand total to $337 billion, or more than $1.5 trillion according to the dollar value in the 1970s.

To attempt to estimate the war's cost solely in monetary terms is of questionable value for it fails to take into consideration humanitarian concerns. There is truly no way to measure the deaths and suffering or the decreased earnings of a crippled soldier or civilian in the years that followed the signing of the armistice. Even today, over half a century later, the total continues to increase as interest due on debts that will never be paid continues to grow, as do the pensions paid to veterans and their dependents.

Few people, however, concerned themselves with figures of war costs in the joyous days of November 1918. The emotional reactions

(1)

to the coming of peace exhausted themselves slowly, and for a few weeks all that had happened seemed unreal. From the heads of state to the men and women in the streets, mental gears had to be shifted. The great and unquestioned goal had been to win the war. Now it had suddenly become how to make the peace.

Two months later the eyes of the world turned toward Paris. There the leaders of the victorious powers would formalize the return of peace. There the representatives of the defeated nations would learn the price they must pay. There, hopefully, sane minds would make certain that the world would never again engage in the insanity of war.

To some it had seemed as if the war was never going to end. Since 1914 they had listened to those who spoke of victory being within reach, if only one more campaign was successful or one more sacrifice made. Yet the war had gone on. By the fall of 1918, however most realistic observers were convinced that Germany and the other Central Powers (Austria-Hungary, Bulgaria, and the Ottoman Empire) were doomed. This seemed obvious as the full weight of American resources, as well as its fresh and eager expeditionary force, became a welcomed reality to the Allied nations of Europe. The nightmare of inevitable defeat became equally real to an increasing number of German leaders. They grasped at the possibility of a peace that might not involve the harsh punishment so often meted out by the victors at the end of a long and bitter war.

In a speech delivered to Congress on January 8, 1918, President Woodrow Wilson of the United States had listed fourteen points as the basis on which peace might be restored. Briefly, the Fourteen Points called for:

> 1. Open covenants (formal, binding agreements) of peace, openly arrived at, after which there shall be no private international understandings of any kind, but diplomacy shall proceed always frankly and in public view;
> 2. Absolute freedom of navigation upon the seas, outside territorial waters . . . except as the seas may be closed by international action for the enforcement of international covenants;

3. The removal . . . of all economic barriers and the establishment of an equality of trade conditions among all the nations consenting to the peace;

4. Adequate guarantees . . . that national armaments will be reduced to the lowest point consistent with domestic safety;

5. A free, open-minded, and absolutely impartial adjustment of all colonial claims, based upon a strict observance of the principle that in determining sovereignty the interests of the populations concerned must have equal weight with the claims of the government whose title is to be determined;

6. The evacuation of all Russian territory, and such a settlement of all questions affecting Russia as will secure for her the independent determination of her own political development and national policy;

7. Belgium must be evacuated and restored;

8. All French territory should be freed . . . and the wrong done to France in the matter of Alsace-Lorraine should be righted;

9. A readjustment of the frontiers of Italy should be effected along clearly recognizable lines of nationality;

10. The peoples of Austria-Hungary should be accorded the freest opportunity of autonomous development;

11. Rumania, Serbia, and Montenegro should be evacuated, and Serbia accorded free access to the sea;

12. The Turkish portions of the Ottoman Empire should be assured sovereignty . . . other nations should be assured autonomous development, and the Dardanelles (strait connecting Europe with Turkey in Asia) should be permanently opened to the ships and commerce of all nations;

13. An independent Polish state should be erected which should include the territories inhabited by indisputably Polish populations, which should be assured a free and secure access to the sea;

14. A general association of nations must be formed under specific covenants for the purpose of affording mutual guarantees of political independence and territorial integrity to great and small states alike.

Since Germany still held hopes of victory at the time Wilson delivered his speech, no response was forthcoming. Nine months later, however, these hopes had vanished, and on October 3, 1918, Germany and Austria-Hungary appealed to the American president for an armistice based on the Fourteen Points.

The German officials addressed their plea directly to Wilson since they feared that a proposal sent to all the Allied governments would be rejected and that German and Austrian lands would be invaded. As a result considerable discussion with Germany took place before Wilson passed on the request to the Allies. Their reply when it came was positive, but they insisted on two reservations. The second of Wilson's points, concerning freedom of the seas, must be eliminated, and Germany must agree to make compensation for all damage done to the civilian Allied population and its property as a result of German aggression on land, at sea, and from the air.

Wilson relayed these conditions to the German government on November 5, 1918. No written reply came, but agreement was obvious when the Germans contacted the Allied commander, Marshal Ferdinand Foch, and accepted his terms for an armistice. Wilson's note thus became a kind of nonbinding contract between the opposing powers. However, the vagueness of many of its terms, especially concerning the question of reparations, made it the basis for innumerable arguments in the months and years to come.

Whatever reservations the German leaders may have had about the negotiations and Wilson's proposals were, however, academic. The conditions existing in the German nation, from the capital city of Berlin to the collapsing armies along the western front, made any decision other than acceptance an impossibility. On November 3 the German fleet at Kiel mutinied. Four days later, Bavaria, second largest of the German provinces, had overthrown its state government and proclaimed itself a republic. (In the chaotic days that followed the end of the war this attempt to introduce a democratic government failed. Early in 1919 its leader, Kurt Eisner, an Independent Socialist, was murdered by the Communists, who seized power until they too were overthrown a few months later.) Even the commanding generals were unable to promise the German emperor, William II, that the armed forces were still loyal to the monarchy.

Unable to find any reasonable alternative, the emperor decided on surrender. On the morning of November 8, in a railroad car located in the French forest of Compiegne, members of a German

Armistice Commission listened to Marshal Foch as he read the provisions agreed upon by the Allies. (In that same railroad car during World War II, Adolf Hitler forced a defeated French nation to do likewise.) The German government was given seventy-two hours to accept or reject the armistice terms. When they accepted at 5 A.M. on November 11, the marshal gave orders for a cease-fire to begin on the western front six hours later. Thus, at the eleventh hour of the eleventh day of the eleventh month of 1918, peace returned after fifty-one months of bloodshed.

Ironically, many of the Allied leaders were unhappy that the armistice had come. General John Pershing, commander of the American forces in France, was one who wished to see the war continue long enough so that Germany itself could be invaded. However, the great majority, including President Wilson and marshals Foch and Henri Philippe Petain of France and Douglas Haig of Great Britain, could see little sense in continuing the struggle, especially considering the terms of the armistice that the Germans had accepted. Its thirty-five clauses included provisions that might be found in any armistice agreement, such as the immediate evacuation of all Allied territory still in enemy hands. There was also much to please those desiring harsher treatment for Germany. Clearly the voices that called not only for an end to hostilities but for the need to punish and cripple the hated "Huns" were being heard. Many of their demands were included in the armistice agreement, and would appear again in the final treaty. For example, Allied forces were to occupy a huge section of German territory along the west bank of the Rhine River, along with bridgeheads at Köln (Cologne), Coblenz, and Mainz.

The armistice also required the surrender of huge quantities of war materiel, including all submarines and 1,700 airplanes. Within two weeks 5,000 locomotives, 150,000 railway cars, and 5,000 motor lorries (trucks) must also be transferred. The treaties of Bucharest and Brest-Litovsk, in which the Rumanian and Russian governments had surrendered to Germany, were voided. All Allied prisoners of war were to be repatriated at once, without reciprocity. Perhaps worst of all to most Germans, the blockade which kept out badly needed foodstuffs and medical supplies, as well as materiels of war, was to continue indefinitely.

The economic as well as the political situation in Germany was fast sinking into complete chaos. As the monarchy crumbled in November 1918, so did the ability of the nation to maintain the flow of dwindling food supplies to the people. The leftists of all stripes blamed the new-born German republic for the semi-starvation that was spreading over the land as winter began. Food soon became a political lever with which the enemies of the government hoped to effect its overthrow. The Allied leaders were aware of these conditions, and the American Relief Administration had already succeeded in lifting the blockade from the liberated countries of east-central Europe. Only in the case of Germany was it continued.

In mid-January, two months after the armistice had been signed, the Allied Council of Ten agreed that Germany had a legitimate need for foodstuffs until the next harvest. It was proposed that the Germans receive 200,000 tons of breadstuffs, along with 70,000 tons of pork products. The eighth article of the armistice itself, which was renewed for the second time on January 16, 1919, stated that these supplies would be forthcoming if Germany would surrender its passenger and cargo fleets. Anglo-American efforts to speed this exchange were, however, constantly blocked by the French, whose program called for keeping the Germans economically on a subsistence level for at least one generation, preferably for two or more. With revenge and punishment clearly foremost in their minds, the French raised two objections. First, they opposed any guarantee that would weaken the blockade as an effective instrument of intimidation and pressure. Second, they vetoed an Anglo-American scheme to have

Above: Allied commander Marshal Ferdinand Foch (left), shown with General John Pershing, commander of the American forces in France, ordered the cease-fire that ended World War I. Below: a view of the centuries-old German city of Coblenz (now in West Germany).

Germany pay for imports with securities and gold otherwise earmarked for future reparation payments.

By March 5, at a conference in Spa (Belgium), the German delegates renewed their pleas with more success. Humanitarian concerns by this time were reinforced by fears that recent leftist uprisings would soon succeed in overthrowing the German government. French delaying tactics were pushed aside. The matter was taken from the second echelon Supreme Economic Council and moved directly to the Council of Ten. There on March 7–8 the issue was thrashed out.

Lord Robert Cecil, the chairman of the Supreme Economic Council, submitted a draft proposal providing immediate delivery of the agreed-upon 270,000 tons of foodstuffs, and permission to allow Germany to import 370,000 tons of food monthly until September 1. Herbert Hoover spoke for President Wilson in support of the measure. British Prime Minister David Lloyd George agreed, but French Minister of Finance Louis-Lucien Klotz remained adamant. In one of the angriest outbursts out of the many that would occur among the Allies during these months of negotiations, Lloyd George personally attacked Klotz and appealed over his head to French Premier Georges Clemenceau. Seeing France totally isolated from the other nine delegations, the French decided to retreat, and Cecil's draft proposal was accepted. The final agreement was signed in Brussels, Belgium, on March 13–14. Germany promptly began delivery of its merchant ships to Allied control, and made their first payment on March 22. Simultaneously, Herbert Hoover diverted several cargoes to German ports. The first to arrive docked in Hamburg on March 25 with 6,600 tons of wheat flour. By the end of May, 380,000 tons of foodstuffs had been supplied. Unfortunately, for almost five months the civilian population, especially women and children, had suffered the various effects of malnutrition and semi-starvation.

How much the harsh armistice terms and the blockade influenced what was taking place at Versailles, and just how much those events determined the history of the next few decades is impossible to establish in full. Certainly they foretold a treaty based on humiliation and vengeance. They would also provide Adolf Hitler at a later date with an invaluable piece of propaganda when he preached his doctrine of hatred against Germany's former enemies.

Such was the situation in Europe during the winter of 1918–19. The "war to end all wars" was over, but already fresh threatening clouds began to appear on the horizon. The victorious nations, each busy preparing its own plans for the postwar world, began to lose affection for those who did not agree with their demands and desires. The defeated nations were disillusioned as hopes faded for fair and just treatment by those to whom they had now surrendered. The delegates who gathered in Paris for what would be the greatest conference in a hundred years sensed the bitter debates and arguments that were to come.

The Organization of the Paris Conference

With the signing of the armistice, discussion in Europe had turned to a consideration of where and when the peace treaties would be negotiated. Even this seemingly simple decision proved complicated. Germany and Bulgaria presented no problem, but Austria-Hungary and the Ottoman Empire, as they had previously been known, no longer existed. Without Allied sanction Hungarian nationalists had repudiated the 1867 agreement that created the "dual monarchy" and were demanding to be treated separately from the Austrians. This empire, which the Hapsburgs had ruled for generations, would now be dealt with by the Allies, if they so agreed, as the new nations of Austria, Hungary, Czechoslovakia, Poland, and Yugoslavia. Other sections of the empire were passing under the control of Rumania and Italy. A similar eruption was taking place in the non-Turkish sections of the Ottoman Empire. For obvious reasons none of these new political creations wanted to be treated in Paris as a defeated "enemy."

The question of where the negotiations should take place also caused discord. The United States and Great Britain favored small cities such as Geneva or Lausanne in neutral Switzerland, but the French insisted on Paris. Forty-eight years earlier they had suffered a humiliating defeat in the Franco-Prussian War. The citizens of Paris had watched a Prussian army march down the Champs Elysées and under the Arc de Triomphe. On January 18, 1871, Bismarck and the German princes had proclaimed the birth of the German Empire in the Hall of Mirrors of the Versailles Palace. Now the tables were turned, and the French had every intention of repaying their hated enemy in kind. The first meeting of the conference was called on the same day in January as the 1871 conference had been, and when the treaty was completed the Germans would be forced to sign it in the same Hall of Mirrors.

How different a setting this would be when compared to the peace conference that had taken place—known as the Congress of Vienna—a century before in 1815. At that time a defeated France stood at the mercy of its Russian, Prussian, Austrian, and British conquerors. The deposed Emperor Napoleon was exiled to St. Helena, and the restored King Louis XVIII was treated, at least formally, as a friend rather than an enemy. France was indeed made to pay for losing the war, but nowhere did one find the hatred, the desire to exact the last ounce of humiliation, and the calls for revenge so prevalent in the Paris of 1919.

So it was that the peace conference came to Paris, and the German treaty would be dealt with at Versailles. The other Central Powers were assigned to other palaces in the suburbs of Paris. Austria would sign its treaty at St. Germaine en Laye, Hungary at Trianon, Bulgaria at Neuilly, and the Ottoman Empire at Sèvres. (The overthrow of the government of Sultan Mohammed VI, who had sent the delegation that signed the Treaty of Sèvres on August 10, 1920, blocked ratification and eventually resulted in a brand new treaty being negotiated in Lausanne, Switzerland, which was not signed until July 24, 1923.)

A less partisan and more practical reason for the choice of Paris was the obvious need for a city large enough to accommodate the huge numbers of people who for one reason or another wished to be present or take part in the negotiations. Twenty-seven of the fifty-three Allied and associated powers sent representatives, along with their staffs of secretaries, advisers, and servants.* Each of these nations demanded at least one hotel large enough to serve as its own headquarters. A major power like Great Britain required five. In addition, vast numbers of journalists and writers arrived to witness the event. Finally, there was an amazingly large group of individuals who appeared on the scene demanding to be heard as they spoke for new nations or groups who were seeking aid in a struggle to win freedom and independence from some oppressing master. Thus, Czechoslovakia, only recently formed from the defunct Austro-Hungarian Empire, sent its leader and future foreign minister Eduard Beneš. From the kingdom of Serbs, Croats, and Slovenes (later to be known as Yugoslavia) came Nicola Pashich, who four year earlier had been prime minister of Serbia. An Armenian delegation pleaded for aid against the age-old persecution of its people by the Russians and Turks. Dr. Chaim Weizmann spoke out for the Zionist movement, reminding the Allied leaders of earlier pledges of support in favor of a Palestinian homeland for Jews. Greece sent Eleutherios Veni-

---

* The official roster of the "Allied and Associated" powers at the Paris Peace Conference totaled twenty-seven. In addition to the five major powers, Great Britain, France, Italy, Japan, and the United States, were:

Belgium, Bolivia, Brazil, China, Cuba, Czechoslovakia, Ecuador, Greece, Guatemala, Haiti, The Hedjaz, Honduras, Liberia, Nicaragua, Panama, Peru, Poland, Portugal, Rumania, The Serb-Coat-Slovene State, Siam, Uruguay.

Note that eleven were Latin American nations wanting to court favor with the United States. Bolivia, which had severed relations with Germany, had not formally declared war.

zelos, who had opposed his own pro-German king during the war. Musician-statesman Ignace Jan Paderewski came to play the piano in the interests of world harmony and Poland. Estonians, Lebanese, Siamese, and two Koreans were among those demanding hearings at the conference table.

When it had become obvious that little or no progress could be made in such chaos and confusion, a Council of Ten was established. It was composed of two representatives each from the United States, Great Britain, France, Italy, and Japan. The Council was to be aided by some fifty-eight committees and commissions that were set up to deal with specific problems. The five major powers were represented on each of them, and, in fact, most of the work of the conference took place there. The general, or plenary, meetings attended by all the delegates became meaningless. After the first one on January 18, attended by seventy delegates and plenipotentiaries along with a large number of substitutes, only five others were called. When they did meet, little discussion or debate took place. Instead, the decisions of the Council, or later of the "Big Four" (omitting Japan), were transmitted to the other delegations. Many of the less important Allies were not much better informed throughout the conference than were the defeated Central Powers. For example, it was not until May 6, the day before the completed treaty was presented to the German delegation, that all the member nations of the conference received the same document.

The Council of Ten quickly proved to be almost as inefficient as the plenary sessions had been. For a month unsuccessful efforts were made to speed up the work of the conference and to block the constant leaking of confidential material. Then, on February 14, the conference was temporarily suspended while President Wilson and Prime Minister Lloyd George returned to their respective homelands for visits lasting four weeks. Upon their return it was decided that the Council of Ten should be abolished, and such action was taken on March 24. From that time on the major work of the conference was conducted by the Big Four—the chief spokesmen of the United

States, Great Britain, France, and Italy. The Japanese government, which thereby lost its voice in making key decisions at the conference table, was not upset over that fact since it had little direct interest in most of the items under discussion. As long as its wishes concerning the fate of German possessions in the Far East and China were respected, Japan cared little about how other issues were settled. As a result, President Woodrow Wilson, Prime Minister David Lloyd George, Premier Georges Clemenceau, and Premier Vittorio Emanuele Orlando became the key figures at the conference, and most of the major decisions were made by this group.

During the Big Four's meetings in April, another temporary reduction in the size of this body took place. Wilson and Orlando became involved in a heated dispute over Italy's right to annex the Austrian port of Fiume, which Wilson felt ought to go to Yugoslavia. He appealed over Orlando's head to the Italian people. The furious Orlando immediately returned to Rome, where he asked the Chamber of Deputies to give him a vote of confidence. It did so by a ten-to-one margin, and shortly he returned to Paris. By that time, however, the Big Four were now functioning quite efficiently as the "Big Three." Since Clemenceau spoke excellent English (which Orlando did not), even the services of an interpreter were no longer required. The frustrated Orlando discovered that his apparent support at home faded rapidly, for only a few weeks later, on June 19, his ministry was overthrown.

The Big Three meanwhile were drawing heavily on the reports of the fifty-eight committees and commissions that, in the course of the four-month conference, held over 1,600 meetings. Here, indeed, was one of the major faults of the conference, for each committee tended to operate completely independent of the others. Had a way been found to increase the exchange of knowledge and views, it is possible that some concessions and modifications of adopted policies and decisions would have taken place. Instead, the great mass of the committees' recommendations were accepted with little hesitation by Wilson, Lloyd George, and Clemenceau. This is not to say that the

three leaders were derelict in their duties, as much as to point out how impossible it was for any three people to consider and evaluate carefully the enormous amount of material being provided for them in such a short period. Some recommendations were never seen, others were ignored, and many were handled with such dispatch that their effect was negligible to say the least.

It is also important to note that in organizing the conference no provision was made to hear the pleas and opinions of the defeated Central Powers. In striking contrast to the great Congress of Vienna in 1815, in which defeated France had played a major role in the discussions that were responsible for the redrawing of the map of Europe, not one oral or written statement by the governments of Germany, Austria, Hungary, Bulgaria, or the Ottoman Empire was allowed before the treaties with those nations were completed. Psychologically, this may have helped to speed up the growth of dissension among the Allies. The very presence of a German spokesman would have acted as a constant reminder, to those beginning to draw apart, of the bonds of comradeship forged in the blood and sacrifice of the recent holocaust. Moreover, the veil of secrecy drawn around the actions of the Big Three resulted in key policy decisions remaining unknown even to many of the conference participants until there was little or no time left for even their protests.

The first of Wilson's Fourteen Points had called for "open covenants of peace, openly arrived at." Instead, the conference organization allowed three aging and overworked men sitting in President Wilson's study in the Place des États Unis to hear all the evidence

Above: the Austrian delegation listens to the terms of its peace treaty at St. Germaine en Laye. Below: the Big Four in conference: left to right, Italian Premier Vittorio Emanuele Orlando; British Prime Minister David Lloyd George; French Premier Georges Clemenceau; and United States President Woodrow Wilson.

presented to them by the committees and commissions. When disputes arose, they and they alone would act as judge and jury.

The Big Four

By far the most dynamic of the Big Four leaders in Paris was Georges Clemenceau. Born in 1841, he spent some time as a correspondent in the United States during the Civil War. Returning to France, he switched from journalism to politics, and later entered the Chamber of Deputies, where he served from 1876 to 1893. In these early days Clemenceau was a member of the radical left, and fought for many social and political reforms that were eventually realized. He battled for the separation of church and state, opposed government censorship, and joined those who supported Alfred Dreyfus, the French army officer accused of treason in 1894. In 1893 Clemenceau's career almost came to an end when his name was linked to a financial scandal involving a company established to build a canal in Panama. He survived, was then elected to the Senate, and from 1906 to 1909 served for the first time as premier. Now, however, he was known as "the Tiger," or still later as "Père la Victoire" (father of victory). An aging and cynical man, he had but one cause left—his passionate belief in the greatness and destiny of France.

Clemenceau's country had called upon him once more in the dark days of 1917 to take the reins of government, and this unquestioning nationalist had responded. Although the war then seemed all but lost, no one doubted his sincerity when he roared defiance. "I wage war," he proclaimed. "Before Paris I wage war. Behind Paris I wage war. If we retreat to the Pyrenees, I shall continue to wage war."

To Clemenceau the true purpose of the Paris peace conference was a twofold one. His beloved France must be made secure forever against the hated Germans. The invasions he had personally witnessed in 1870 and 1914 must never happen again, and to make

(16)

certain of this, Germany must be permanently crippled. He believed that French influence over Europe was logical, inevitable, and just. From the start, therefore, he quarreled with Lloyd George, and more particularly with Wilson, both of whom held quite different concepts of the aims and objectives of the conference. In his biting and sarcastic way, Clemenceau once remarked, "Lloyd George thinks he is Napoleon, but President Wilson believes himself to be Jesus Christ." On another occasion he is said to have commented, "Even God was satisfied with Ten Commandments, but Wilson insists on Fourteen!"

Clemenceau's years of experience and vast knowledge of world affairs served him well, however, and he was clearly one of the outstanding diplomats at the conference. He rarely underestimated opponents, and often preferred to avoid direct confrontations with them. In Wilson's case, for example, Clemenceau paid lip service to the high purposes and idealistic statements made by the American leader, while, in fact, working diligently toward his own goals, which were in direct contradiction.

Although he won many victories at the conference table, total success escaped him. Only a year later, in 1920, when he stood as a candidate for the presidency of the republic, his own countrymen turned away and elected another. Retirement followed, and Clemenceau died in 1929.

In contrast to the forceful French premier, Vittorio Emanuele Orlando, the fifty-nine-year-old Italian leader who had become prime minister in October 1917, was unquestionably the least impressive member of the Big Four. Not only was his nation far less powerful than the other three major Allies, but Orlando personally suffered the handicap of being unable to understand the English language spoken so fluently by his three colleagues. The net result was that, for the most part, his comments and advice were politely listened to and ignored. Had Italy possessed the wealth or power of the other three, the term "Big Four" would certainly have come closer to the reality of the situation. In fact, Italy was in no position to overrule any decision agreed upon by Britain, France, and the United States. The implication that Orlando played a role of any importance was a sop to Italian pride, as was the constant use of the label "Big Four."

In one respect, however, Orlando was like his French counterpart. He cared little or nothing for Wilson's idealistic principles. His only real aim was to win for Italy all and more than had been promised. In the 1915 secret treaty of London, certain pledges had been made to the Italian government if it would forsake its neutrality. Orlando had no intention of letting the British and French forget that agreement. His excessive demands finally led to an open break with Wilson, who opposed Orlando's claims to the Austrian port of Fiume. As we know, when Orlando left for home to rally support for his stand, the Big Three continued to work in his absence. When he returned, they did not seem overly impressed by the vote of confidence he had received. On June 19, he fell from office, but this made little difference since the issues most directly concerning Italy had already been settled. On June 2 the Austrian delegates had been handed the completed draft of the agreement, which they had no choice but to accept and sign. Since the spoils of victory desired by Italy would come primarily from the Austrian nation, Italian interest in the other treaties diminished considerably. It would be accurate to say that Orlando was remembered more as an irritant at the Paris peace conference than as one of the chief architects of the new world order created there.

If Wilson and Clemenceau can be said to represent the extremes present at the Paris conference (idealism versus self-interest), then Prime Minister David Lloyd George of Great Britain held the middle ground. Twenty-two years younger than his French colleague and seven years Wilson's senior, this fierce, energetic Welshman, head of his country's Liberal party, by no means played a secondary role among the Big Three. More often than not he held the deciding vote, and so on many issues his support determined what provision went into the treaty. His quick mind, his background in law, and the experience he had gained while serving in such positions as member

Premier Clemenceau, followed by
Marshal Foch, reviews troops at Dover.

of the House of Commons, president of the Board of Trade, chancellor of the exchequer, minister of munitions, secretary of state for war, and since 1916 prime minister proved invaluable. Like Clemenceau, he also had a sense of humor.

Among Lloyd George's faults were a distaste for minor details, which he constantly overlooked, and indifference to the fact that on numerous occasions he reversed himself. Yet, one great advantage he had over his colleagues was a superior day-to-day knowledge of all aspects of the conference. This was due to the excellent system of reporting that he set up in the delegation. All British representatives on all committees were required each evening to write a report on what had happened during the day. These were rushed to central headquarters at the Hotel Majestic. There copies or summaries were prepared, mimeographed, and then rushed to all British representatives and staff, including, of course, the prime minister.

Lloyd George saw his role as quite different from that of his fellows. Great Britain by tradition had always been opposed to allowing any one nation to dominate the European continent. Philip of Spain, Napoleon, and most recently Kaiser Wilhelm II had learned that to their dismay, and now Clemenceau had to be taught the same lesson. The shrewd Lloyd George had no intention of allowing the hold over Europe that the French now hoped to establish. He did agree that the Germans must be punished, but in moderation. He held this attitude in spite of the fact that his success in obtaining a majority of over 250 seats in the House of Commons in the election of December 1918 had come in good measure because of the campaign slogans that he and the Liberal party had used. "Hang the Kaiser" and "Make Germany Pay!" were typical. Nevertheless, he believed enough in the balance-of-power principle to use his influence against any total destruction of Germany. Aside from that one belief, he was as determined as Orlando and Clemenceau for Italy and France, respectively, to win for Great Britain the largest possible share of the spoils.

The final and perhaps most important member of the Big

Four was the twenty-eighth president of the United States, Woodrow Wilson. Standing apart and at times in opposition to almost all of the delegates who attended the conference was this unique and complicated man. Hindsight has convinced many that he was a hero with feet of clay, or perhaps no hero at all, but it is undeniable that in 1919 he was a towering giant among men to millions of people all over the world. When he arrived in Europe to attend the conference, enormous crowds welcomed him everywhere. His receptions in London, Paris, and Rome were unprecedented. The leaders of the Allied nations might, at least in private, be sarcastic about the American schoolteacher president, but Italian peasants burned candles before his portrait, and even the peoples in the defeated Central Powers saw in him the only opportunity for obtaining fair and decent treatment at the conference table. No mere citing of numbers can convey the hysterical, delirious, enthusiastic support he found everywhere he traveled.

Everywhere, that is, except back home in the United States. There, to a considerably smaller number of people, Wilson was the champion of a universal, just, and enduring peace, and to far more a controversial president and the head of a political party. Wilson had entered the White House in 1913 only because the Republican party had been split between Theodore Roosevelt and William Howard Taft. He thus became the second Democrat to serve since the Civil War. His second victory, in 1916, had been such a close one that his rival (Republican Charles Evans Hughes) had gone to bed election night believing that he had won. The margin of victory, no matter how narrow, had given Wilson the power, however, and he was well prepared to use it to the fullest. Domestically, he did so with the help of a Democratic majority in Congress. Then, just as the war ended, he, like Lloyd George, faced an election, but where the British prime minister was rewarded by winning, Wilson's good fortune failed him. Congressional elections in 1918 for the entire House of Representatives and one third of the Senate were required according to the Constitution. The president called upon the people to

*The American delegation, with Wilson
seated in the center, at Versailles*

elect a Democratic Congress to assist him in winning the peace as they had helped in winning the war. The unfair implication was that somehow Republicans had not done their share in the war effort and the nation responded by electing the Republican party to majority positions in both houses. Even then Wilson did not seem to grasp the message. When he sailed for Europe on the *George Washington*, December 4, 1918, virtually the entire delegation accompanying him was Democratic. Henry White, a wealthy and retired former ambassador to France, was the only one of the president's senior advisers who was a Republican, and he had little influence or standing in his own party. There were suggestions that former President Taft or Senator Henry Cabot Lodge, the chairman of the Senate Foreign Relations Committee, be included in order to give a bipartisan flavor to the delegation, but the president was adamantly opposed.

These actions on the part of Woodrow Wilson say much about the personality of the man, who in spite of his brilliance could and did make the most incredible errors of judgment. Born in Staunton, Virginia, in 1856, he was raised in a religious household. His father was minister of the First Presbyterian Church; his mother was the daughter of a minister. Wilson left home some years later for a year at Davidson College in North Carolina, a small Presbyterian school, then attended Princeton University, the University of Virginia Law School, Johns Hopkins University, and Bryn Mawr, where he studied and taught. Not until 1910, when he was fifty-four years old, did he hold a political office, becoming the governor of New Jersey. If this background is kept in mind it becomes easier to understand why he acted so differently from the great majority of those who sat in positions of power in Paris. Wilson was still much more the morality-minded political science professor than the practical politician. This proved to be both a blessing and a curse. The high moral tone and scholarly manner that were so characteristic of him frequently made it difficult for him to be understood by the general populace, or at least that part of it which did not accept on faith much of what he had to say. It also cost him the friendship of many who worked with him, when they failed to appreciate his own rigid principles as well as his inability to compromise on basic beliefs.

Another handicap was Wilson's poor health. The demands of the American presidency are considered overwhelming in normal times, and doubly so in times of war. The president's delicate health was simply not up to the task of acting as the nation's chief executive, Democratic party leader, and chief diplomat and negotiator all at the same time. He was constantly on the verge of total exhaustion, and actually did much of his work during this period while confined to bed.

Finally, it must not be forgotten that Woodrow Wilson was not an expert in the field of foreign affairs. Although a brilliant scholar, it is significant that his major published work was in the area of American governmental organization. When he first entered the White House, he had expected to concern himself primarily with domestic matters and, until the outbreak of the war and America's growing involvement in it, such was the case. Unlike Clemenceau, Lloyd George, and even Orlando, Wilson arrived in Paris with no definite program in mind save only a rough draft of a covenant for a League of Nations. On this point alone he was a virtual fanatic. Time and time again he would tire of the protracted discussions and arguments and give way on another violation of his ideals or on another of the Fourteen Points. However, he never weakened in his determination to see the covenant of the League of Nations completed and to make certain that it was made an integral part of the treaty. His clever colleagues soon realized this, and won concessions from him in return for pledging their support for the league. The president, as he saw himself agreeing to points contrary to all his beliefs and principles, clung to the hope that once the League of Nations was "a *fait accompli* nearly all the serious difficulties would disappear." Even more revealing was his remark made after the conference had ended and he had returned to America: "I would never have done what I did if I had not been sure that the League of Nations would reverse that decision."

The Territorial
Provisions
of the Treaty

When the Allied leaders settled down to begin the actual drafting of
the treaty provisions, nothing involved more discussion and intense
concern than the revision of the borders of Germany. No one doubted
that changes would be made, but enormous argument followed over
whether they should be based on the national interests of the countries involved or on the principles expressed by Wilson in the Fourteen Points.

France, speaking through Clemenceau, immediately demanded
and received the provinces of Alsace and Lorraine. They had been
surrendered at the close of the Franco-Prussian War of 1870–71,
and for the past forty-eight years it had been the chief objective of
French foreign policy to create the conditions that would force Germany to return them. (It is for this reason more than any other
that historians give France a major share of the blame for causing
World War I. More than any other power, the French had a clear-
cut motive for desiring a general European war, for without it the
chances of regaining the provinces of Alsace and Lorraine were
negligible. In an isolated Franco-German war, all signs pointed to a
repeat of the 1871 victory by the Germans. Only when allied to
Great Britain or Russia, or both, could this most precious of all
French foreign policy goals be achieved.) The great majority of those
living in the twin provinces, which lie between France and Germany,
probably preferred to live in France, and there is no question that in
Lorraine the culture and traditions of the area would logically have
made it French.

The French premier, however, demanded more. The area known
as the Rhineland (including 10,000 square miles on the west bank
of the Rhine up to the Dutch, Belgian, Luxembourg, and French
borders) was German by tradition, culture, language, and choice. It

ATLANTIC

OCEAN

NORTH SEA

NORWAY

SWEDEN

FINLAND

Oslo

Stockholm

Helsinki

Leningr

BALTIC SEA

Tallinn
ESTONIA

Riga
LATVIA

DENMARK
Copenhagen

SCHLESWIG

Kiel

Memel
LITHUANIA

Dublin
IRELAND

GREAT
BRITAIN

London

NETHERLANDS
Amsterdam

Hamburg

Elbe

Stettin

GERMANY

Oder

Berlin

Gdynia
Danzig

POLISH
CORRIDOR

EAST
PRUSSIA

Allenstein

Neman R.

Vistula

Warsaw

POLAND

Brussels

Malmedy

THE
RHINELAND

Köln (Cologne)

BELGIUM

LUX.

Aachen

Weimar

SILESIA

R.

Paris
Versailles

Mainz

ALSACE
and
LORRAINE

SAAR BASIN
BAVARIA

Rhine R.

Prague

CZECHOSLOVAKIA

Vienna

BES

FRANCE

Lausanne

Geneva

AUSTRIA

Budapest

HUNGARY

RUMANIA

Bucharest

PORTUGAL

Madrid

SPAIN

Lisbon

ITALY

Rome

Belgrade

YUGOSLAVIA

Danube River

Sofia
BULGARIA

ALBANIA
Tirane

GREECE

Athens

MEDITERRANEAN SEA

Geo. Buctel

Areas affected by the Versailles Treaty

0   200   400   600

Miles

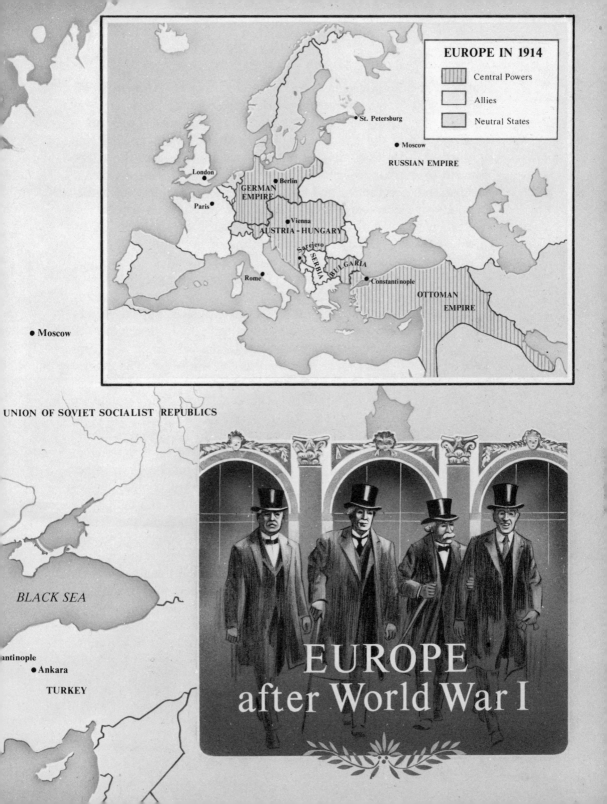

EUROPE IN 1914

Central Powers
Allies
Neutral States

St. Petersburg

Moscow

RUSSIAN EMPIRE

London

GERMAN EMPIRE

Berlin

Paris

Vienna

AUSTRIA - HUNGARY

Sarajevo

SERBIA

BULGARIA

Rome

Constantinople

OTTOMAN EMPIRE

Moscow

UNION OF SOVIET SOCIALIST REPUBLICS

BLACK SEA

antinople

Ankara

TURKEY

EUROPE after World War I

contained some of Germany's greatest cities, such as Aachen, Köln, Coblenz, and Mainz, as well as considerable industry and huge reserves of coal. Using the argument that nature intended the German border to end at the river's edge, French President Raymond Poincaré and Marshal Foch insisted that Clemenceau work for the establishment of a separate Rhineland state that France could dominate. To that end, the French and Russians had earlier signed an agreement. Lloyd George and Wilson refused to permit such a partition, the former because it would have made France too strong and Germany too weak, the latter because it violated his belief in the right of self-determination by the people in the area.

In his eighth point, Wilson had called for the return of Alsace and Lorraine to France, but beyond that he would not go. After bitter, protracted negotiations, it was finally decided that the Rhineland would be occupied by Allied troops for a number of years. A northern sector, including a bridgehead to the east bank, was centered about Köln. It would be occupied for five years. The central sector, based on a similar bridgehead at Coblenz, would be held for ten years, and the southern sector centered about Mainz for fifteen years. In addition, a strip of territory along the east bank of the river to a depth of 50 kilometers (or about 31 miles) must be kept permanently demilitarized along with the rest of the Rhineland. Any failure on the part of Germany to fulfill all the other provisions in the treaty would result in permanent occupation of the Rhineland. Then, Clemenceau added, both Britain and the United States must sign supplemental guarantee treaties. In them, the French border would be guaranteed protection against German aggression. Only when this demand was granted did the Frenchman finally drop his demand for a separate Rhineland state, which could have constituted a permanent "buffer zone" between these two traditional enemies.

The discussions concerning the Rhineland also involved a 723-square-mile subdivision known as the Saar Basin. At the time it contained a population of 660,000. In the year before the war began, the Saar had produced 17 million tons of coal, which equaled 40 percent of the entire French production. Its reserves were estimated at 17 billion tons, more than all the reserves of France, and 20 percent of the prewar German reserves. This area was also German beyond question, so its annexation by France was again blocked by Wilson, with support from Lloyd George. The compromise this time was to establish a committee of British, French, and Americans, who some time later came up with the following solution: they (1) transferred to France the ownership of all the coal mines and their accessories; (2) included the Saar within the French customs and monetary union; (3) allowed the setting up of French-speaking schools for the miners' children; (4) put the government of the Saar under a commission chosen by the League of Nations; (5) provided that after fifteen years a plebiscite or referendum be held, with voting restricted to men and women over the age of twenty who had lived in the territory at the time the treaty was signed, which would permit them to decide the future sovereignty of the area (provided that a vote to return to Germany would then require the League of Nations to set a price on the coal mines before they were given back); and (6) that the value of the coal removed by the French during the twenty-year occupation by the League of Nations be credited to Germany's reparation account. Here was a classical example of the severity of the treaty terms that would cause not only immediate bitterness but continued tension for the next two decades.

A bit farther to the north, along the Belgian border, another vote was held in three small but strategic areas known as Eupen, Malmédy, and Moresnet. Holding but 70,000 inhabitants, they were desired by the Belgian government primarily to "straighten" its frontier. The German government was not permitted to play any role in the election, and the area voted for union with Belgium.

Along the northern border where Germany and Denmark touch, the future of the province of Schleswig was also determined by a plebiscite. There the result saw the cession of the northern half of the province to Denmark, while the southern half remained with Germany.

The eastern border saw the greatest changes of all. The German port city and territory of Memel at the mouth of the Nieman River was ceded to the Allies. At that point they were not sure what to do with it, since both the new states of Poland and Lithuania laid claim to it. In January 1923, Lithuania ended the dilemma simply by occupying the area. The following year a convention signed by Lithuania, France, Great Britain, Italy, and Japan legalized the seizure in the name of the League of Nations. No plebiscite was permitted.

In his thirteenth point, Wilson had called for an independent Polish state with a free and secure access to the sea. His proposal was carried out by forcing Austria and Russia, as well as Germany, to give up the Polish-speaking areas that these three nations had held since the 1790s. In the case of the German cession, the new frontier lines resulted in cutting the nation into two parts. For the next twenty years the ceded area would be known as the famous Polish Corridor and would poison relations between the former and present owners. The Corridor was composed of West Prussia and most of the province of Posen, which were given directly to Poland. This area, some 260 miles long and up to 80 miles wide, had an extremely mixed population (a town might have a clear-cut German majority, for instance, while the surrounding countryside might be populated by a clear-cut majority of Poles), and under the best of conditions it would have been almost impossible to draw up what both sides would have agreed to as a fair settlement. However, the fact that at least a third of those living there—many in local districts that were as much as 75 to 90 percent German—showed how little the principle of self-determination counted. Two other districts in East Prussia were allowed to hold a plebiscite. Allenstein voted to remain German. Marienwerder split, with the larger half going to Poland.

Along the southwest corner of the new Poland, the frontier

*A view of the
coal-rich Saar Basin*

touched the rich German province of Silesia. Parts of what was known as Lower Silesia were handed over to the Poles. They were, however, anxious to gain the coal, lead, and zinc mines in Upper Silesia, although the area was predominantly German. Once again a plebiscite was held. In spite of the intimidation of a Franco-Italian occupation force, the vote favored Germany 700,000 to 480,000. Poland refused to accept the outcome, and fighting broke out. The British and French tried unsuccessfully to work out a compromise, so the problem was eventually passed on to the council of the League of Nations. It left Germany with more than half the land and population, but gave 53 of 67 coal mines, 9 of 14 steel and rolling mills, all of the zinc and lead foundaries, 11 of 16 zinc and lead mines, and 75 percent of the coal-producing areas to Poland. Another new nation, Czechoslovakia, obtained without a plebiscite a tiny area of Upper Silesia called Hultchin.

At the mouth of the Vistula River sat the ancient Hanseatic city of Danzig. A historic center of German trade and commerce since it became powerful and famous in the Middle Ages, it was now detached from Germany to become a "free city" under the control of the League of Nations. Poland was granted certain special diplomatic and economic rights, but not outright possession. This was a good example of the fact that the vengeful, makeshift, and unjust provisions of the treaty did not, and could not, work. The Danzigers themselves were unhappy for the next twenty years. When the Nazi movement in Germany arose and promised eventual annexation of the city, most of its inhabitants were quick to join. The Poles, who had failed to win its annexation, proceeded to build up the nearby inferior coastal town of Gdynia. One result was economic depression in Danzig for two decades. The fate of Danzig, as an example of what the Versailles Treaty did to Eastern Europe, was completed on September 1, 1939. On that day the armies of Adolf Hitler, beginning World War II, could attempt to justify their aggression against Poland by claiming that they were simply regaining Danzig and freeing the persecuted Germans who were living in the Polish Corridor.

Finally, there was the problem of what to do about the German colonial empire. Not having achieved unification until 1871, the Germans were latecomers in the rush of European imperialists to partition much of the rest of the world. Although Otto von Bismarck, the great chancellor who set German foreign policy until 1890, had never been an enthusiastic supporter of colonial possessions, by the time World War I broke out Kaiser Wilhelm did rule over a goodly number. The most important were in Africa, with Tanganyika or German East Africa being the largest and most valuable, along with the Cameroons, Togoland, and Southwest Africa. In the Far East was the port of Kiaochow located on the Shantung Peninsula in China, half of the island of New Guinea called Kaiserwilhelmsland, and a number of small Pacific islands. Under the guise of removing them from the oppressing rule of Germany and turning them over to the League of Nations, the Allies actually enlarged their own empires. Once again one of Wilson's Fourteen Points proved an embarrassment. Point five had called for "a free, open-minded, and absolutely impartial adjustment of all colonial claims, based upon a strict observance of the principle that in determining all such questions of sovereignty the interests of the population concerned must have equal weight with the equitable claims of the government whose title is to be determined." That meant that open annexation was virtually impossible. Only in the cases of Kiaochow and the Shantung Peninsula were no attempts made to hide the blatant imperialism. Japan seized the area in total disregard of the wishes of the Chinese inhabitants and the sensibilities of Woodrow Wilson. World opinion, however, was strong enough to force Japan to pledge that the area would eventually be returned to China, which it was in 1945.

All other German colonies were officially ceded to the League of Nations and were henceforth called "mandates." The Class A group was made up of those territories taken away from Turkey and said to be nearly ready for independence. Class B mandates were rated in need of continuing "supervision," with self-government a remote possibility. Class C mandates were considered so small or

sparsely occupied as to be better off attached to larger nearby political units, although still subject to certain vague rules of the League of Nations that would safeguard the rights of the indigenous population. All of the German colonies were rated as B or C mandates. As B mandates the British gained Tanganyika (except for the small Ruanda-Urundi area in the northwest corner, which was attached to nearby Belgian Congo), one sixth of the Cameroons, and one third of Togoland. The remainder of those two colonies went to France. In the C mandate category were Southwest Africa, which was turned over to the Union of South Africa; Kaiserwilhelmsland to Australia; the island of Samoa to New Zealand; and Nauru (rich in phosphates and now a small independent island nation) to joint rule by Britain, Australia, and New Zealand. The remainder of the German Pacific islands were divided along the equator, those to the north going to Japan and those to the south to Australia.

The Versailles Treaty thus took from Germany, often in direct violation of the letter and spirit of the Fourteen Points, one eighth, or 25,000 square miles, of its territory and all of its colonies. The population of about 70 million was reduced by over 6 million. The areas lost included over 15 percent of the arable land, 12 percent of the livestock, and 10 percent of the factories; 72 percent of the zinc reserves, 65 percent of the iron ore, 57 percent of the lead, and 45 percent of the coal resources were also removed. The complicated organization of trade, commerce, banking, and industry in this great industrial nation was crippled. When all the other political and economic restrictions placed on Germany are also taken into account, the reasons for the total collapse of the German economy within three years are hardly surprising.

Above: Adolf Hitler used one result of the Versailles Treaty to begin World War II.

Below: Tanganyika was once a German colonial possession.

Military Restrictions, Economic Provisions, and Reparations

In the discussions concerning disarmament, Allied hypocrisy was perhaps more evident than when territorial changes were made. After what became routine statements in favor of the idea that all nations should now disarm, the delegates did nothing except to strip the defeated powers of their remaining military establishments, and then plan how best to keep them in a state of permanent inferiority. Wilson's fourth point called for the reduction of national armaments "to the lowest point consistent with domestic safety," but it was applied only to Germany. A limit of 100,000 men, including no more than 4,000 officers, was placed on its army. To prevent a rapid turnover that could build up a huge reserve, enlistments had to be voluntary and for a period of twelve years for the men and twenty-five years for the officers. Conscription (drafting) at any time was forbidden. The treaty listed the exact number of guns, rifles, cannon, ammunition, tanks, armored cars, and other equipment permitted. The manufacture of war materiel was limited, as was the amount that might be stored "at points to be notified to the Governments" of the Allies. No war materiel was to be imported or exported. So that an army could not be built up under cover of other duties or titles, the number of customs officers, forest rangers, and coast guardsmen was frozen at the 1913 figure. The police forces were also limited to expansion only in relation to population growth.

The German navy was restricted to six old-style battleships, six light cruisers, twelve destroyers, and twelve torpedo boats. No submarines were allowed. For purposes of replacement, no ship was to be built in excess of 10,000 tons. All ships above the allotted number were to be turned over to the Allies or destroyed. Naval personnel was limited to 15,000 men and 1,500 officers, with term enlistments similar to those of the army. The naval base on the island of Heligoland was to be dismantled, as well as all fortifications within 50 kilometers of any part of the German coast.

No German air force of any sort was permitted. All existing planes and materiel were to be turned over to the Allies or destroyed. To make sure that these and the other military provisions would be carried out, an inter-Allied control commission was set up. Germany would pay the full cost.

Economic restrictions were just as severe. Among the most notable were the separation of Luxembourg from the German customs union, the granting of "most favored nation" treatment for five years without Allied reciprocity, acceptance of confiscation of all property held in foreign countries, including that of individuals, with no compensation other than what they could gain from their own government. Other clauses established an international commission to control the Rhine, Elbe, Oder, Nieman, and Danube rivers. The Kiel Canal was internationalized, and Czechoslovakia was given a "free zone" in the harbors of Hamburg and Stettin.

Hindsight shows that the most bitterly controversial part of the Versailles Treaty was Part Seven, which dealt with reparations. Had all the other provisions in this enormous document of 15 parts, 440 articles, and scores of annexes been half as vindictive, there can be no doubt that as soon as it was possible Germany would have begun endlessly protesting this section. Before listing what the prostrate German nation would have to pay, Part Seven laid down its legal and moral justification for reparations in Article 231, which stated:

> The Allied and Associated Governments affirm and Germany accepts the responsibility of Germany and her allies for causing all the loss and damage to which the Allied and Associated Governments and their nationals have been subjected as a consequence of the war imposed upon them by the aggression of Germany and her allies.

Known as the "war guilt" clause, it was followed by Article 232, in which Germany promised to make complete reparation for all losses and damages. An annex listed the categories, which included everything possibly connected with the war, pensions and allowances to veterans as well. Germany was also to pay Belgium a sum equal to all that nation had borrowed from other Allies during the war, plus five percent interest.

A reparations commission was to determine the final sums due, and set up the payment schedules, which in no case would allow Germany to pay less than the full amount within thirty years after May 1, 1921. In the interim year the government was to pay in advance in gold, ships, securities, and produce the equivalent of $5 billion. From this sum would be withdrawn the amount needed to pay for the cost of the army of occupation, with the balance credited to the German reparation account.

It would be almost impossible to list the details of the reparation part of the treaty. One example that is typical of the degree to which instructions were given can be seen in the case of merchant ships. The Allies were entitled "to the replacement ton for ton and class for class, of all merchant-marine ships and fishing boats lost or damaged owing to the war." Germany must, therefore, surrender all vessels of 1,600 tons or more, one half of those between 1,000 and 1,600 tons and a quarter by tonnage of all steam trawlers and fishing boats. On demand of the reparations commission, Germany must also build new ships for the Allies up to 200,000 tons a year for five years.

Another case was coal. Out of the reduced reserves (and not including production from the mines of the Saar Basin) each year for ten years, Germany must deliver 7 million tons to France, 8 million to Belgium, and over 7 million to Italy. France would, in addition, get "annually for a period not exceeding ten years an amount of coal equal to the difference between the annual production before the war of the coal mines of the Nord and Pas de Calais, destroyed as a result of the war, and the production of the mines of the same areas during the years in question: such delivery not to exceed 20 million tons in any one of the first five years, and 8 million tons in any one year of the succeeding five years."

Immediate delivery within three months of 500 stallions (three to seven years), 30,000 fillies and mares (eighteen months to seven years), 2,000 bulls, 90,000 milk cows, 1,000 rams, 100,000 sheep, and 10,000 goats were among other items on the list of things to be sent to France, with lesser amounts of each going to Belgium. The ultimate was probably reached with the order that the German government restore to His Majesty the King of the Hedjaz the original Koran of the Caliph Othman, which the Turks had presented to Kaiser Wilhelm II, and that it "hand over to His Britannic Majesty's Government the skull of the Sultan Mkwawa, which was removed from the Protectorate of German East Africa." (The point here is not that the copy of the Koran and the skull of the sultan were unimportant to the Arabs, but rather the degree to which the conference concerned itself with relatively minor provisions whose aims were as much to humiliate Germany as to provide justice.)

The reparations commission, whose task it was to total up the full bill, consisted of representatives from Great Britain, Italy, Belgium, and France. The chairman (the French delegate) was empowered to break any tie vote, and often did so when Britain and Italy opposed some of the more extreme demands of the French and Belgians. A German offer to pay $25 billion over a lengthy period of time was ignored. Finally, on April 28, 1921, it came up with the figure of $33 billion, plus the total war debt of Belgium, as the price that Germany must pay. American financial experts calculated that this was double the amount Germany was capable of paying. During this same period another conference was held in the town of Spa to decide how the spoils should be divided. The result was to give France 52 percent of everything collected, the British Empire 22 percent, Italy 10 percent, Belgium 8 percent, and the remaining 8 percent to be split among all other claimants.

The incredible thing about these demands is that the so-called experts drawing them up could not see that the beaten, dismembered Germans could not possibly fulfill them, even if they had had the will to do so. Instead, at a later meeting the reparations commission

considered raising the grand total to $56 billion. Germany did meet the first installment early in 1921, but only at the cost of starting a serious monetary inflation cycle that, within two years, left it in total default, the economy in shambles, the currency worthless, and with an army of French, Belgians, and Italians marching across the Rhine to occupy the industrial district of the Ruhr. Such punishment did little good, and all the detailed provisions concerning reparations suddenly became meaningless.

Even without the reparation payments it was questionable whether or not the German economy could have avoided complete collapse. These payments would simply aggravate an already serious situation brought on by the human and material losses of four years of warfare, the cession of much of Germany's mineral and industrial wealth, the breakdown of international trade, the absence of foreign credits, and even the government's inability to repay the 98 billion marks that it had borrowed from its own citizens during the war. Germany now entered a period of chaos from which Adolf Hitler was to emerge as the champion of those who would seek the destruction of the rest of the Versailles Treaty.

The League of Nations

The first part of the Versailles Treaty consisted of the Covenant of the League of Nations. The idea for an international body of nations joined together to preserve the peace of the world was by no means a new one, but few of its advocates had had the power and oppor-

Above: the harsh terms of the Versailles Treaty
brought great economic hardship to an already
weak Germany. Here armed workers march through
the streets of Berlin in protest against the economy.
Below: shortly after the Versailles Treaty, Germany
was in economic collapse. This family in Essen
struggles to survive in overcrowded quarters.

tunity possessed by Woodrow Wilson in 1919 to try and make it a reality. As far back as 1915 the American president had remarked that the war, which the United States had not yet entered, must not end before the setting up of an organization that would outlaw such conflicts in the future. This theme appeared again and again in his remarks and speeches. Then, on January 18, 1918, in his address to the United States Congress, it became the last and most famous of the Fourteen Points. It read: "A general association of nations must be formed under specific covenants for the purpose of affording mutual guarantees of political independence and territorial integrity to great and small states alike."

Wilson knew that he would face opposition in his struggle to fulfill this dream of a perpetual peace based on the principles of legality and morality and operating under the guidance of a League of Nations more concerned with justice than national aspirations. Yet when he sailed for Europe on December 4, only eleven months later, he was full of hope. In Paris, despite the tumultuous greetings he had received everywhere, the opposition was waiting in the form of Clemenceau and Lloyd George. First they tried to use delaying tactics, proposing to deal with the political, economic, and territorial issues before turning to the question of a League covenant. The president realized, however, that if this happened the chances for the League were few indeed. Once the spoils of war had been shared, it was quite probable that the Allied leaders would pack their bags and rush home. By sheer determination Wilson had his way. The League of Nations must come first, and it did. At the second plenary session on January 25, 1919, Wilson was appointed chairman of a committee to draft the covenant. Aiding him in its preparation were men from fourteen nations. He leaned mostly on Jan Christian Smuts of South Africa, Leon Bourgeois of France, and Robert Cecil of Great Britain, as well as on his own staff. Twenty days later, on February 14, 1919, he proudly presented the completed covenant to the fully assembled delegates. There was considerable criticism, and twenty-six changes were made before it was finally adopted on April 28, becoming the first twenty-six articles of the Versailles Treaty.

A period of relative calm followed. Lloyd George and Wilson both returned to their homelands to deal with domestic problems, while Clemenceau was busy recovering from a wound inflicted by a would-be assassin. When the Big Four gathered again on March 14, the meetings were devoted to more practical problems involving border changes, reparations, and the like.

We have already seen how troubled the president became as he saw the treaty become an instrument of vengeance and oppression. Yet he always clung to the hope that whatever evils were committed could later be corrected by the League of Nations. The covenant had said that the primary purpose of the new organization was "the promotion of international cooperation and the achievement of international peace and security." It would, therefore, be more than just an instrument for preventing war. It would be an agency for common action on problems of common concern to the whole world. All self-governing political units, whatever their age, size, or importance, were to be members of the Assembly, in which each would have one vote. Here, Wilson felt, the voice of world opinion would be heard; and what nation could stand against it in defense of a bad cause? To aid the Assembly there would be a smaller Council, in which the executive functions of the League of Nations were vested. The Council had permanent seats allotted to the major powers of the world—the United States, Great Britain, France, Italy, and Japan—and four others that would be filled annually by the other members of the League. With its concentrated power, Wilson believed that it could act quickly when the occasion required and carry out the will of the Assembly.

In addition to the Assembly and Council there would also be a Permanent Court of Justice. At its headquarters in the Peace Palace at The Hague in the Netherlands, fifteen judges would sit as an international tribunal. These men were to be chosen by the Assembly and Council, and they would be expected to represent all the peoples of the world rather than just those in their native lands. They would become the arbitrators of disputes among the nations of the world, who then could have no reason to resort ever again to armed conflict.

It is not too difficult to understand why President Wilson did not see the extent of his failure to win a just and lasting peace at Paris. No one enjoys facing up to the collapse of his or her fondest hopes and dreams. Wilson's clever mind and wounded conscience quickly sought out and found an escape from this obvious conclusion. The petty and vindictive provisions, such as Article 227, which called for a personal vendetta against the former German emperor who must be tried "for a supreme offense against international morality and the sanctity of treaties," could be put aside under the label of "unfortunate but minor." Even those errors of undeniable importance could be faced, for the very treaty that perpetuated them also provided a means short of war for their correction. All of Wilson's misgivings and despair were balanced by the creation of a League of Nations whose job would be to right these wrongs. It seems incredible, at least in retrospect, that he could have so deluded himself, but considering his defense of the finished treaty there is no doubt that he did.

In all fairness to those who opposed the whole idea of the League of Nations, it should be pointed out that the new world organization proved to have a number of very substantial defects, some of which the opponents noted long before history proved them correct. The veto power given the great powers, the lack of any independent source of revenue other than that gained by appeals to the membership, no military force of its own, the absence of the Soviet Union (whose Communist government was to be for some years isolated from the family of "respectable" nations), Germany and the other defeated nations—not to mention the United States as it rather

Above: the first assembly of the League of Nations, 1920; below: the League's 1930 assembly in Geneva.

ironically turned out, since the American Congress later voted against joining the League—were a few of the troublesome omens. So too was the refusal to include a suggested amendment offered by Japan. In it was confirmed the principles of the equality of all nations and just treatment of all their nationals. Racial prejudice and fear that it might justify a movement for unrestricted oriental immigration caused Great Britain and Australia to lead the fight against the amendment. Such signs did not indicate too clearly that creation of a League of Nations meant the coming of the millennium.

The German Response

After the signing of the armistice on November 11, 1918, the German people and their leaders watched with growing concern the actions of the victorious powers, into whose hands they had surrendered themselves. During the next few months, however, their attention was constantly distracted by the extraordinary events taking place at home.

Throughout most of the war the German Empire of Kaiser Wilhelm II was run by his appointed Chancellor (prime minister) von Bethmann Hollweg, who occupied that office from 1909 to July 1917. His failure to bring the war to a successful conclusion led to his dismissal, although a number of successors were unable to do any better. Finally, in October 1918, Prince Maximilian of Baden became chancellor. A liberal noble who hoped to introduce widespread reforms that might save the tottering monarchy, he included in his cabinet two leaders of the powerful Majority Socialist party, Gustav Bauer and Philipp Scheidemann. These men, along with Gustav Noske and Frederick Ebert, were the most important figures in the party that would soon take over the reins of government.

The Social Democratic party of Germany was made up of moderate reformers who positioned themselves somewhere between the Conservative and Catholic parties on the right, and the Bolshevik, later called Communist, followers of Karl Marx on the left. The party had unfortunately split in the early part of 1916 over the question of support for the war effort. The Majority Socialist wing continued its support, but others led by Hugo Haase broke away and formed the Independent Social Democratic party. By 1918 these Independent Socialists, as they were now called, became somewhat more radical on other issues and were demanding rapid nationalization of industry. They did not, however, go as far as the extreme radicals or Sparticists (named after the pen name of their Bolshevik leader Karl Liebknecht, who had written and published articles signed "Spartacus"), who were advocating immediate establishment of a proletarian dictatorship.

In any case, by the end of October 1918, Majority Socialist leaders like Noske and Scheidemann had joined in the growing public demand that Prince Max force the kaiser to abdicate. When, on November 9, Field Marshal Otto von Hindenburg agreed that this was the best course of action, Wilhelm II realized the hopelessness of his position. He prepared to renounce his crown, and early on the morning of November 10 fled to the Netherlands, which permitted him to live in quiet exile until his death in 1941. With his full and official abdication on November 28, 1918, the German Empire ceased to exist.

Meanwhile, on the day of Wilhelm's flight, Prince Max, having received a pledge from Frederick Ebert that law and order would be maintained and that an assembly would be called to prepare a new constitution, surrendered the powers of government into Ebert's hands. At this point (and at the very time the armistice was being signed in France) the empire was thus converted to a federation of republican states, provisionally ruled by a Council of People's Commissars. Composed of three Majority Socialists, including Ebert and Scheidemann, and three Independent Socialists, led by Haase, its authority was immediately challenged by the Sparticists.

Both the Independent Socialists and the Sparticists hoped to postpone the election of delegates to a constituent assembly, since they believed that more time was needed to increase their popular support.

(47)

However, a national congress of councils made up of organizations of soldiers and workers, which had sprung up all across the land, met in December and set the date for January 19, 1919 (the day after the first general meeting of the Paris conference). The Sparticists reacted by planning an uprising before the election. During the week of January 5 the revolt came, and for almost ten days Germany hovered on the brink of a civil war that could have led to the establishment of a Communist dictatorship. Led by Noske, the Council of People's Commissars fought back. By January 15, the day on which both Karl Liebknecht and Rosa Luxemburg, the two leading Sparticists, were arrested and killed on the way to prison, the revolt was crushed.

On January 19 the general election was held in an atmosphere of relative quiet. Thirty of 35 million eligible voters went to the polls to choose among the candidates of half a dozen parties. The Social Democrats (the Majority Socialists had reclaimed their old name) won 163 of the 421 seats. To achieve a majority in the assembly they quickly moved to form a coalition with the 88 Christian Democrats (formerly the old Catholic, or Center, party), led by Matthias Erzberger, and the 75-man delegation of Democrats (whose support had come from the old left-wing National Liberals and Progressives), led by the brilliant banker Hjalmar Schacht. The opposition to this coalition thus held 95 seats. It included 22 Independent Socialists, 21 People's party delegates (chiefly businessmen who were formerly right-wing National Liberals whose outstanding leader Gustav Stresemann would later serve for many years as the foreign minister of the Weimar Republic), 10 minor party members, and 42 reactionary Nationalists, who spoke for the old Conservative party and all those who wished to re-establish the monarchy.

The Council of People's Commissars announced that the newly elected assembly would meet in the small peaceful city of Weimar on February 6. There it elected Frederick Ebert as the first president of the German Republic. Scheidemann became chancellor and Count

Brockdorff-Rantzau, who had no political affiliation, was appointed foreign minister. It was to these men that the call from Paris came on April 18, 1919.

Having completed the drafting of the treaty in less than four months, the Allies were now anxious to present it to the Germans. Their note spoke of the treaty being "received" by the German representatives. Berlin replied that three officials would be sent to pick it up and bring it back. A second note the next day was somewhat more conciliatory, and by asking that the plenipotentiaries be sent, it implied that negotiations would take place. After a further exchange of clarifying notes, Count Brockdorff-Rantzau, five other delegates, and a staff of 174 prepared to leave for France.

The fact that these German representatives had been political opponents of the kaiser and his reactionary militaristic supporters, and that they did not even speak for the German Empire that had fought the war, made no apparent impression upon those sent to receive them. When the Germans arrived at Versailles on April 29, they were rudely treated. Isolated at the Hôtel des Réservoirs, once the palace of Madame de Pompadour, they never saw or heard from their opposite number for five days. Only a threat on their part to return to Berlin brought action. A French liaison officer said that the conditions of peace would be handed to Brockdorff-Rantzau on May 7, 1919, at three o'clock in the afternoon at the Trianon Palace Hotel at Versailles. When the agenda for this confrontation arrived, the Germans were even more shocked. No oral discussion would take place, and Germany was given up to fifteen days to present, in English and French, its written observations on the whole of the treaty.

At the appointed hour, the six Germans and their two interpreters met the representatives of the Allied and associated nations. Premier Clemenceau faced them, flanked on the right by Wilson and on the left by Lloyd George. With biting sarcasm the French leader began by addressing the delegates of the German Republic as "Messieurs les delegues de l'Empire allemand."

"This is neither the time nor the place for superfluous words. You have before you the accredited plenipotentiaries of the great and lesser Powers, both Allied and Associated, that for four years have carried on without respite the merciless war which has been imposed upon them. The time has now come for a heavy reckoning of the accounts. You have asked for peace. We are prepared to offer you peace."

Following his remarks, a volume of the conditions of peace were handed to the Germans. Count Brockdorff-Rantzau then replied. He and his staff had spent considerable time on what might be the only occasion on which the two sides would sit across a conference table. Answering in German, he began:

"Gentlemen, we are deeply impressed with the great mission that has brought us here to give the world forthwith a lasting peace. We are under no illusions as to the extent of our defeat and the degree of our powerlessness. We know that the strength of the German arms is broken. We know the intensity of the hatred which meets us, and we have heard the victor's passionate demand that as the vanquished we shall be made to pay, and as the guilty we shall be punished."

In the remainder of his address he repudiated the war-guilt clause, maintained that the basic cause of the war had been fifty years of imperialism and expansion, and asked for a nonpartisan committee to study the whole question of responsibility. In discussing the problem of reparations, he pointed out that exaggerated claims would bankrupt Germany, bring economic chaos to Europe, and incidentally make it impossible for creditors to obtain even legitimate claims.

Much was made in the press of the fact that the German spokesman remained seated while delivering his reply. A large percentage of the journalists in Paris and throughout the world were still engaging in typical, wartime, hysterical ravings about "the Huns." To them, this horrendous action proved beyond doubt the indestructible arrogance of the Germans. It was learned years later that Brockdorff-Rantzau had questioned Commissioner General Walter Simons on this very point and had been told that it was a matter of personal choice.

As a diplomat of many years experience, it is probable that Brockdorff-Rantzau felt it beneath his dignity to stand as if he were a common criminal before the bar of justice. In any case, the speech itself was not favorably received. Clemenceau scowled throughout its delivery and appeared several times as if he were going to interrupt. Wilson listened carefully. Almost all of the press were hostile, but it must be said in their defense that, since the terms of the treaty had not yet been made public, it was difficult for them to understand why the Germans were acting as an injured party.

The German staff was now faced with the need to translate quickly the 440 articles of the treaty, which totaled some 80,000 words. When the job was completed and the contents reviewed, the assembled delegation by a unanimous vote refused to accept it unless fundamental changes were made. President Ebert and his cabinet back in Berlin came to the same conclusion. He sent instructions to the delegation that a protest be submitted in which the provisions were to be denounced as "unfulfillable, unbearable, and ruinous." Brockdorff-Rantzau toned down the protest somewhat, stating only that it was impossible to meet some of the demands, as would be explained in a series of specific notes to be submitted in the immediate future. He also showed how many of the points in the treaty lacked the legal basis that the two sides had agreed upon before and during the armistice. Clemenceau replied that the treaty did not violate previous understandings or the Fourteen Points, and that in any case Germany would not be permitted to protest the fundamental assumptions to be found in that document. Only "practical suggestions" would be considered.

Told that any general criticism was unacceptable, the Germans tried a new approach. The treaty was examined down to the last detail, and a flood of single notes and papers protesting point after point flowed onto Allied desks. It all proved to no avail. From May 9 to May 28 only a few changes were permitted. For example, Germany would be admitted to the International Labor Office preceding

any possible admission to the League of Nations itself. Also, should the Saar Basin in fifteen years vote for reunion with Germany, payment for the coal mines was not required to be made in gold.

There remained now but one last hope for the German delegation. A statement could be made when they returned the treaty and their answer to the Allies. It was decided to prepare a comprehensive memorandum on the contents of the treaty as a whole. Every effort was then made to see that what would be a final appeal for justice showed the German arguments in their best light. Even members of the cabinet took part in the preparation, meeting with some of the delegates in Spa, about halfway between Versailles and Berlin. A covering introductory note was written by a leading newspaper correspondent, Dr. Guttmann of the *Frankfurter Zeitung,* whose journalistic style, it was hoped, would appeal to the general public.

The first part of the memorandum, entitled "General Remarks," was written by Walter Schücking, an eminent professor of international law who later would become a judge in the Permanent Court of International Justice. His section dealt with the pre-armistice negotiations and promises made by the Allies, and concluded that, "All this shows that the draft of a Peace Treaty as submitted to the German Government stands in full and irreconcilable conflict with the basis agreed upon for a just and durable peace." The second part consisted of a legalistic and concise enumeration of the proposals already submitted in the single notes. Eleven subdivisions were needed to outline those parts of the treaty that were considered acceptable and those in which revision was requested. No emotional appeal was made, the demands were moderate, and great faith was placed in the role of a League of Nations. For example, disarmament was accepted unconditionally, and an offer to pay reparations to the amount of

Above: the German delegation at Versailles; Count Brockdorff-Rantzau stands fourth from the left. Below: the German people turn out in mass protest.

$25 billion was made if Article 231 was withdrawn and Germany was permitted again to enter world trade markets.

So much time was consumed in putting the German counter-proposals together that when they were submitted on May 29 only the covering letter had been translated into English and French. The memorandum itself required 443 large printed pages, as compared to the 230 needed for the treaty itself!

The Allies then put ten committees to work on a reply. Lloyd George, whose position had become increasingly less vengeful and far more moderate the longer the conference continued, now joined in urging for some revision of the treaty. He seems to have been impressed by some of the German arguments, and also was beginning to believe that the treaty as it then stood would probably lead to at least the economic collapse of Germany. Among the American delegates even stronger protests were being heard, and in fact one major modification of the treaty had won approval. The direct cession of Upper Silesia to Poland was denied unless upheld by the local inhabitants in a plebiscite. Other changes might also have been included but for the fact that most of the committees and commissions had already dissolved. The French had made it clear that few if any further changes would be tolerated without bitter opposition on their part. Certainly the acceptance of any new unsupported German protests would be little more than a formality. Many experts had left for home, leaving those still in Paris to work with the secretariat in preparing the answers. Since a high proportion of this technical staff was French, and since that country's full delegation was available, the conference host put its advantage to good use. No further concessions were made.

Finally, on June 16, after three more weeks of isolation, the Allied reply was delivered to the German delegation. Aside from a few other minor alterations nothing had changed. Germany, said the covering letter, had not only planned the war, but was responsible for the savage and inhuman manner in which it was carried out.

Unconditional acceptance of the treaty was demanded within five days. Failure to do so would mean immediate invasion.

The German delegation then requested and was granted a two-day extension, since it would take the members that length of time to return home and report to their government. On the way back to Berlin, Commissioner General Simons wrote a statement that was signed by all the chief delegates. It recommended that the government refuse to sign the treaty.

The reaction to the terms of the treaty within Germany had been changing since they were first disclosed on May 7. Just five days later the National Assembly had returned from Weimar to Berlin, where it now held a meeting in the largest auditorium at the University of Berlin. The leaders of every major party present rose to denounce the terms. Chancellor Scheidemann was followed by Hermann Müller, who led the Social Democrats. Adolph Gröber spoke for the Catholic Center party, Conrad Haussmann for the Democrats, and Dr. Gustav Stresemann for the German Volkspartei, to name but a few. Only the Independent Socialists and the Communists, who believed that imminent world revolution would make the treaty meaningless, failed to add their voices to the roar of protest that sounded across the entire country. It seemed for a moment as if Germany would find the strength to renew the war rather than submit.

During the next eighteen days, however, cold hard facts slowly replaced those emotional daydreams. Germany simply did not have the strength to resist. To try and do so would mean only that the slaughter would begin again, with absolutely no chance of success. By June 18 the delegates had arrived from Versailles calling for the rejection of the treaty, but the heart had already gone out of those who two weeks earlier had shouted defiance. The cry of "We shall not sign" had become the whisper of "We must sign." On June 19 the three major parties in the coalition government polled their members. The Social Democrats voted 75 to 35 to sign. The Democrats stood 55 to 0 against. The vital Center party tried to compromise by voting to sign provided the Allies eliminated articles 227 to 231. These were the provisions dealing with the surrender of certain "war criminals" who must stand trial and the accusations that Germany had violated the code of war, along with the war-guilt clause. Even then, sixteen members of the party voted against signing. With his coalition government deadlocked, Chancellor Scheidemann resigned. So did Count Brockdorff-Rantzau and Walter Simons, both of whom retired from government service. The same day, June 20, Field Marshal Paul von Hindenburg was admitting that further military resistance on the western front was an impossibility. On the twenty-first another Social Democrat, Gustav Bauer, became chancellor. Before he was able to form a cabinet another day had passed, and only twenty-four hours remained before the Allied ultimatum would run out.

On the morning of the twenty-third, the National Assembly met again and for three hours debated Bauer's motion to accept the treaty if articles 227 to 231 were removed. It carried by a vote of 237 to 138. The government immediately communicated the information to Paris, only to be told later that such a conditional acceptance would not do. The Bauer cabinet was now stunned, for Matthias Erzberger, a leader of the Catholic Center party, chairman of the Armistice Commission, and member of the coalition government, had given them assurances that his contacts with Allied officials indicated their willingness to rescind the five articles. Another message was sent to Paris requesting a forty-eight-hour extension, but this was denied. At seven o'clock the Allies were still preparing to order their troops to advance across the Rhine.

A hasty meeting of the Catholic Center party was called and a new vote taken. This time it went 64 to 14 against signing. Chancellor Bauer again met with the National Assembly, now to ask permission to sign the unrevised treaty. Bitter debate raged for an hour. At last, with the vote of enough members of the Catholic Center, the motion carried. The decision was telegraphed to Paris barely two hours before the ultimatum expired. This last message to the Allied command read in part:

> The government of the German Republic is overwhelmed to learn . . . that the Allies are resolved to enforce . . . the acceptance even of those provisions in the treaty which . . . are designed to deprive the German people of their honor. . . . The German people, after their terrible sufferings during these last years, are wholly without the means of defending their honor. . . . Yielding to overpowering might, the government of the German Republic declares itself ready to accept and to sign the peace treaty imposed by the Allied and Associated governments. But in so doing the government . . . in no wise abandons its conviction that these conditions of peace represent injustice without example.

It was difficult to find anyone at this moment willing to go to Versailles to sign the treaty. The humiliating task finally fell to Foreign Minister Hermann Müller and Colonial Minister Johannes Bell. They too were treated like prisoners upon arrival, and were showered with stones and verbal abuse as they left Paris for Versailles.

At three o'clock on June 28, the anniversary of the day in Sarajevo when the assassination of the Archduke Francis Ferdinand sparked the outbreak of the Great War, the Germans entered the Hall of Mirrors. They were the first to sign the treaty, followed by the Allied leaders in alphabetical order in French. President Woodrow Wilson led as he signed for *Amérique du Nord*.

The German surrender was complete. The war was formally over.

Conclusion

The Versailles Treaty is one of the major tragedies of the twentieth century. It ended a war in which millions of people fought and died in the belief that they were defending their homelands against unjustified aggression, believing slogans that spoke of "the war to end all wars" and "the war to make the world safe for democracy." Moreover, the most powerful of the nations involved was led by a man who deeply believed that these idealistic objectives could actually be achieved. Why then did everything turn out so badly? Why did the treaty poison the relationship between wartime allies, embitter the people of the defeated nations even more than they already were, fail to fulfill the words of its own preamble, which called for the replacement of the state of war "by a firm, just and durable peace," and end by becoming a major factor in bringing about a more destructive world war only twenty years later?

There are numerous answers to these questions. Some of them contradict each other. Over half a century later, historians continue to argue, not so much about what actually took place, as about what should have been done by those who made the decisions in Paris in 1919.

The key figure in the story has always been Woodrow Wilson. For the first two years of the Great War he was the champion of American neutrality, and as late as the fall of 1916 won re-election to the presidency as his supporters proudly shouted, "He kept us out of war!" Then, in a matter of months, the lover of peace became a great war leader. He mobilized the wealth and manpower of the United States and used it to break the stalemate of almost four years that existed between the Allied and Central powers. Then in less than a year Wilson appeared in yet another role. This time he became the idolized hero of vast numbers of men and women of good will who believed that he alone could bring good out of the evil of war. Now he was the champion of the League of Nations, whose creation would outlaw man's greatest folly—war—forever.

The criticism leveled at Wilson comes from opposite directions. French nationalists in particular accuse him of sentimentality and fuzzy thinking. They maintain that Germany was not sufficiently punished due to his interference. Had Allied armies rolled across the German countryside, had an independent Rhineland state been set up, had the "war criminals," including Kaiser Wilhelm II, been tried —so goes this line of reasoning—Germany would never again have reached the rank of a world power. Even if a Nazi movement had then arisen, the nation it would have controlled could never have threatened the rest of the world.

A greater number of critics follow a different line of argument. They see Wilson's failure in his willingness to make concession after concession in every part of the treaty except that dealing with the establishment of a League of Nations. They see as false logic a course of action that permits the seeds of hatred and future conflict to be planted simply because at the same time an institution to undo such wrongs is being set up. That is to say, had Versailles produced a "just and durable peace," the immediate need for a League of Nations was removed. Besides, if a true spirit of justice and reconciliation had permeated the peace conference, it is reasonable to assume that the League covenant would still have been written and adopted.

Such speculation on both sides can never, of course, be proven. Harsher treatment of Germany could easily have pushed its people into the arms of the Communists. Alliance with the new Soviet Union would then have followed; and who can seriously argue that such a course would have guaranteed a peaceful Europe? Or suppose Wilson had been more stubborn in resisting the demands of men like Orlando and Clemenceau? Some say he would have, had his failing health been better. There is still no certainty that he would have succeeded. What then? Would American withdrawal from the conference table have ensured the writing of a fairer treaty? Would the infuriated former friends have written an even harsher treaty without the United States being present? Or would the war have resumed? . . . Hardly a desirable solution . . .

Other students of the treaty pay less attention to the individuals involved. They believe that the failure in Paris was due less to Wilson's idealism or Clemenceau's hatred for Germany than to the organization of the conference. The point made here is that everything connected with the meetings in Paris ensured that a settlement based on vengeance rather than justice would be written there. They mark the contrast with the 1815 Congress of Vienna. There too the great powers of Europe had gathered to redraw the map of Europe, to punish a powerful former enemy, and to provide a means of preserving peace in the future. But in this case the defeated enemy was

(59)

permitted to take part in the negotiations. Far from being excluded, France was represented by the brilliant Talleyrand. This extraordinary man, by 1919 standards, should have been put on trial as a "war criminal," since only recently he had served the hated Napoleon as minister of foreign affairs. Instead, Talleyrand spoke not only for France but in time for many of the smaller Allied nations at Vienna who disliked some of the decisions being made by the great powers. By the time the conference ended, the mark left by Talleyrand was second only to that of Austria's Prince Metternich and Russia's Czar Alexander.

More to the point, a comparison of the results of the two conferences clearly indicates the superiority of the Congress of Vienna. Mistakes were made there too, but that conference did give Europe a century of relative peace before the continent again plunged into a general war. The Versailles settlement lasted only twenty years.

Other critics of the Paris conference try to make a more basic point when they say that the real fault was America's entrance into the war in the first place. Had the United States maintained its neutrality, a negotiated rather than a dictated peace would have been inevitable. Both sides were exhausted by 1918. Neither was in a position to win the war, or for that matter to go on fighting much longer. Without the direct involvement of the United States' armed forces, supplies, and financial aid, Britain and France would have agreed to a very different peace settlement. This argument then concludes that a disillusioned

Above: Clemenceau addresses the German delegation at Versailles, June, 1919. Below: for this happy crowd on Armistice Day, 1918, "the war to end all wars" is over. In a little over twenty years, World War II would begin.

but not desperate Germany would have moved in the direction of a constitutional monarchy rather than into the arms of a Nazi fanatic.

Putting aside such speculation, it is possible to draw at least a few conclusions about the Versailles Treaty. It was a harsh, cruel, and unjust one. The fact that Adolf Hitler made this point over and over again does not make it any less valid. It is also true that, being a treaty of vengeance, it had the effect of lessening or destroying in Germany feelings of remorse and guilt that the people ought to have had about their own behavior in bringing on the war. Among the victors, knowledge of the vengeance at Paris also left its mark. As the years passed guilt grew about the way in which Germany had been treated. Ironically, then, the kind of concessions that should have been made to the democratic-minded leaders of the infant Weimar Republic were instead granted to the National Socialist dictatorship of Adolf Hitler.

The impossible reparations demanded of Germany illustrate another point. They destroyed that nation's economy in less than three years. That fact no doubt pleased those who continued to hate Germany, but at what a cost! When the collapse came, it resembled a whirlpool and dragged the rest of Europe down along with the Germans.

In the treatment of Germany's colonies, another fault appears. The Allies failed to grant the native peoples a voice in their own future, while at the same time proclaiming the rights of self-determination for white Europeans living in Poland, Schleswig, or Alsace and Lorraine. How much anguish, suffering, and blood might have been spared if that right had been freely given by the great powers two or three decades before they were forced to grant it.

Even in redrawing the boundaries of Germany we can observe how the most brilliant men can blind themselves with passion. It is hard to believe that even in 1919 these diplomats could not see that Danzig would not be content to remain a "free city" or that the Saar would wish to rejoin Germany even if, as it turned out, that also meant accepting Adolf Hitler.

Finally, the Versailles Treaty reversed the philosophy of the French and German peoples. From 1871 to 1914 it was France who had cried out against the treatment received at the end of the Franco-Prussian War and for the regaining of territory taken from the French by force. Now this same cry for revenge, revision, and restitution could be heard from the German people. The same might also be said of Austria, Hungary, Bulgaria, and Turkey, all of whom felt they too had been unfairly treated. Here, indeed, were many of the seeds of World War II.

Revenge, it is said, may be sweet, but it is almost always an expensive treat not worth the cost. This is perhaps the primary lesson to be learned from a study of the 1919 Treaty of Versailles.

Bibliography

The following books have been helpful in the writing of *The Versailles Treaty*, and will be of assistance to any reader who wishes to probe deeper into the subject.

Bailey, Thomas Andrews. *Woodrow Wilson and the Lost Peace*. New York: Macmillan, 1944.

Czernin von und zu Chudenitz, Ferdinand. *Versailles 1919: The Forces, Events and Personalities that Shaped the Treaty*. New York: G. P. Putnam's Sons, 1964.

Eubank, Keith. *The Summit Conferences 1919–60*. Norman: University of Oklahoma Press, 1966.

Kessler, Harry Klemens Ulrich. *Germany and Europe*. Port Washington, N.Y.: Kennikat Press, 1971.

Link, Arthur Stanley. *The Impact of World War I*. New York: Harper and Row, 1969.

Luckau, Alma Maria. *The German Delegation at the Paris Peace Conference*. New York: Columbia University Press, 1941.

Lutz, Hermann. *German–French Unity; Basis for European Peace*. Chicago: Henry Regnery, 1957.

Marston, Frank Swain. *The Peace Conference of 1919; Organization and Procedure*. London: Oxford University Press, 1945.

Mayer, Arno J. *Politics and Diplomacy of Peacemaking; Containment and Counter-revolution at Versailles 1918–1919*. New York: Alfred A. Knopf, 1967.

Taylor, A. J. P. *From Sarajevo to Potsdam*. New York: Harcourt Brace Jovanovich, Inc., 1965.

U.S. Department of State. *The Treaty of Versailles and After; Annotations of the Text of the Treaty*. Washington, D.C.: U.S. Government Printing Office, 1947.
(This large volume, which contains the full text of the Versailles Treaty, is invaluable in any possible approach to the subject.)

Index

Allied Council of Ten, 6, 8, 12
Allied Powers. *See* Clemenceau, Orlando, Lloyd George, Wilson.
American Relief Administration, 6
Armistice terms, 4–9
Austria-Hungary, 2, 3, 9

Big Four, 12, 13
    See also Clemenceau, Lloyd George, Orlando, Wilson
Big Three, 13, 15, 16–24
    See also Clemenceau, Lloyd George, Wilson
Bourgeois, Leon, 42

Cecil, Robert, 8, 42
Central Powers, treaty terms, 10–16
    See also Treaty provisions
Clemenceau, Georges, 8, 13, 25, 42, 43, 49, 51, 59
    See also Big Three, Big Four, *and* Treaty Provisions.

Eisner, Kurt, 4

Foch, Ferdinand, 4, 5, 28
Fourteen Points, 2–3, 15, 24, 35, 42, 51
France at Versailles.
    See Clemenceau, Georges.

German delegation to Versailles, 46–57
Germany
    defeat of, 2–9
    economic conditions, 6, 36–41
    military restrictions, 36–41
    reparations due, 36–41
    response to treaty, 46–57
    territories in question, 5, 25–35
Great Britain at Versailles
    See Lloyd George, David

Haig, Douglas, 5
Hitler, Adolf, rise to power, 5, 32, 41, 62
Hoover, Herbert, 8

Italy at Versailles.
    See Orlando, Vittorio Emanuele

Japan at Versailles, 12, 13

Klotz, Louis-Lucien, 8

League of Nations, 24, 29, 30, 41–46, 53, 58, 59
    See also Wilson, Fourteen Points
Lloyd George, David, 8, 12, 13, 28, 29, 42, 43, 49, 54
    See also Big Three, Big Four, *and* Treaty Provisions.

Mandates. *See* Treaty provisions, territorial.

Orlando, Vittorio Emanuele, 13, 59
    See also Big Three.
Ottoman Empire, 9

Pershing, John, 5
Petain, Henri Philippe, 5
Poincaré Raymond, 28

Reparations Commission, 39–41

Revenge, French feelings of.
    See Treaty provisions.

Roster at Versailles, 11–12

Simons, Walter, 50, 56

Smuts, Jan Christian, 42

Supreme Economic Council, 8

Treaty provisions
    economic, 36–41
    German response to, 46–57
    military, 36–41
    reparations, 36–41
    territorial, 25–35

United States at Versailles
    See Wilson, Woodrow.

Versailles, organization of conference at, 9–16

Versailles Treaty, as cause of World War II, 57–63

Vienna, Congress of, compared to Versailles, 10, 59–63

Wilhelm II, 20, 39, 46, 58

Wilson, Woodrow, 4, 5, 8, 12, 13, 28, 29, 42, 43, 44, 49, 58
    Fourteen Points, 2–3, 15, 24, 35, 42, 51
    See also Big Three, Big Four, and Treaty Provisions.

World War I, cost of, 1

About the Author

The Versailles Treaty is a familiar subject to Harold Cecil Vaughan. A student and teacher of history over the past twenty-five years, he has been on the faculty of the Collegiate School in New York City and the Brooklyn Friends School, and now teaches at Ridgewood High School in New Jersey. A native New Yorker, he served in the Army Air Corps after receiving his A.B. degree from Columbia College. He returned to Columbia University after World War II for his M.A. and further graduate study. Mr. Vaughan is a frequent lecturer on historical subjects to the National Society of the Colonial Dames in New York, as well as to the Junior League, the Long Island Historical Association, and the Contemporary Club. His previous books include: The Citizen Genêt Affair, 1793; The Hayes-Tilden Election of 1876; The X Y Z Affair, 1797–98; and The Monroe Doctrine, 1823 (all Focus Books).